C000128226

An insight into forgiveness

An insight into
forgiveness

Ron Kallmier and Sheila Jacobs

WAVERLEY ABBEY INSIGHT SERIES

Published 2008 by CWR, Waverley Abbey House, Waverley Lane, Farnham, Surrey GU9 8EP England. CWR is a Registered Charity – Number 294387 and a Limited Company registered in England – Registration Number 1990308.
Reprinted 2019.

For a list of National Distributors, visit cwr.org.uk/distributors
Unless otherwise indicated, all Scripture references are from the Holy Bible: New International Version (NIV), copyright © 1973, 1978, 1984 by the International Bible Society. NLT: Scripture quotations marked NLT are taken from the Holy Bible, New Living Translation, copyright © 1996, 2004. Used by permission of Tyndale House Publishers, Inc., Wheaton, Illinois 60189. All rights reserved.
Concept development, editing, design and production by CWR.
Printed in the UK by Page Bros
ISBN: 978-1-85345-491-2

WAVERLEY ABBEY INSIGHT SERIES

The *Waverley Abbey Insight Series* has been developed in response to the great need to help people understand and face some key issues that many of us struggle with today. CWR's ministry spans teaching, training and publishing, and this series draws on all of these areas of ministry.

Sourced from material first presented over Insight Days by CWR, presenters and authors have worked in close co-operation to bring this series together, offering clear insight, teaching and help on a broad range of subjects and issues. Bringing biblical understanding and insight, these books are written both for those who help others and those who face these issues themselves.

Where case studies are included, names and details have been changed to protect the identity of the people concerned. Permission has been given for the stories to be told.

Contents

Foreword

While Psalm 23 and 1 Corinthians 13 are frequently read at funerals and weddings, the most quoted scripture throughout the world is Matthew 6: 9–13 – what we know as the Lord's Prayer. Jesus taught His disciples then and now how to pray. Sadly, however, this pattern is often repeated more as a ritual than a prayer, especially that middle sentence '... forgive us our debts as we also have forgiven our debtors'. Or, as we usually pray, 'Forgive us our sins as we forgive those who sin against us'. What is almost always ignored is the poignancy of these words of verses 14 and 15 which underline God's forgiveness when we forgive – and what happens if we don't!

Jesus was teaching that we can be forgiven by God in the same proportion that we forgive others who offend us! That's quite a thought.

This superb book deals with these questions and puts them into topical context.

I have been forgiven much by God, initially as I was born again – and ever since. Within our family we have had to forgive much and we have known the harshest of testings when we willingly forgave the terrorist who was found guilty of killing our Special Branch son. We have experienced real healing when we are able to forgive, even in the smallest of matters; such an attitude deals with bitterness, thoughts of retaliation or the silliness of not speaking to an unforgiven friend. Peace of mind is part of that healing. It is then that we can move on.

Christians have been forgiven much by God and often by others, and having been forgiven, how encouraging that we are accepted by God and by friends, neighbours and even our adversaries.

On the other hand, if we are able by God's grace to forgive others, we are taking on ourselves that which Paul advocated in Philippians 2 verse 5: that our attitude should be the same as Christ Jesus. What better way of following Him who forgave the apostle Peter and so many others in His walk on earth – even forgiving from the cross.

The willingness to forgive, to say sorry and to be forgiven is the basis of life at peace with God, with our family, our neighbours and even those who give us a hard time. The impossible is also possible – loving our enemies – in the strength which God supplies.

I commend this book to you and your friends. Its truths are proven beyond doubt, so let us practise what is preached.

Robin Oake

Introduction

The seeds of this book have been sown over many years. As a pastor and counsellor, I have listened to people of all ages struggle with issues of forgiveness. Many of these people have been victims. Others have been perpetrators. And each of us, if we are honest, will probably agree that during our lifetime we have participated in both roles at various times.

Forgiveness is not an easy matter. It cuts across all our natural desires for justice or revenge. For the victims, it seems too *cheap* to 'just' forgive the offender; on the other hand, for the offenders, there are often consequences of guilt and shame which wrap them up in the suffocating blanket of their failures and sins. How does one undo the past? These issues are our central focus.

For Jesus, the issue of forgiveness was very important. It was so important that He was willing to give up His own life to make the offer of forgiveness available to us. He understands that the journey of forgiveness can be life-transforming.

Over the years I have been privileged to offer a number of seminars that include the topic of forgiveness. In my role as Director of Training at CWR's centre at Waverley Abbey House in Farnham, Surrey, I led a day workshop on this topic. This book is offered to you as a practical guide, and is based upon the seminars and discussions of that workshop.

Additionally, I have appreciated the skill of Sheila Jacobs in picking up the various threads of my workshops and writings, then drawing them together with her own insights to form the easily accessible information you will discover here.

Because this is a practical book, it is our prayer that everyone who reads it and engages with the forgiveness issues it addresses will find the emotional and spiritual release that forgiveness can bring. My stories involve real people, but some facts have been changed to protect confidentiality.

May God bless you in your journey through this book. May you find the freedom of forgiveness afresh in your own life.

Ron Kallmier

If you have read the Gospels, you have probably noticed how Jesus emphasised the importance of a forgiving attitude. You have probably also noticed, from personal experience, that forgiveness is hard!

Many of us have suffered emotionally, mentally or physically as a result of what someone has said or done to us and we find that this has transformed our thinking and personalities. It can seem as if we are stuck in a time warp, a constant loop of thinking back. And, before we know it, we are eaten up with resentment and our lives are defined by that person, that event, that *thing* we can't let go of. We might justify hanging on to our bitterness by saying, 'Do you know what that person has done to me? I can't forgive. It'll be like letting them off the hook.' But we have to realise that forgiveness isn't about letting *them* off the hook, it is about letting *ourselves* off the hook.

Maybe it is ourselves we can't forgive. Perhaps we are constantly thinking about something we said or did that hurt another, and are consequently weighed down by real or imagined guilt. Either way, we can't let go – so we find we can't move on.

The following are questions commonly asked by those who have suffered damage from others or who struggle because they know that they are the offender: 'How can a person forgive?

Is forgiveness an unrealistic goal? Is it only for the virtuous and pious few? What do you do when you find you simply *can't* forgive? Does God condemn us? What about when the damage is caused by the Church, God's own people? What can we do, practically, to forgive someone who has hurt us badly? Can we really ever move on? And what if *I* am the offender?'

In this book, we will explore just why forgiveness is important for our health and wellbeing. We will look at both biblical and psychological perspectives. There are suggested activities, reflections and prayers to help us on our way. And, by the grace of God, as we learn to trust Him with our pain on the difficult journey of forgiving and being forgiven, we will begin to find peace, a fresh start and the freedom Jesus promises to all who follow Him.

Sheila Jacobs

NB If you are coming alongside a person struggling with issues of forgiveness, you may find it helpful to refer to Appendix 2.

CHAPTER 1

Why forgive?

There may be many reasons why you have chosen to read a book about forgiveness. You may be helping a friend struggling to forgive someone for a serious offence, injury or abuse; you may personally be wrestling with issues of forgiveness concerning an injury to someone you love; or you may be on a journey of forgiveness for injuries committed against you – either recently or, perhaps, many years ago. You may equally be on a path to forgiveness but as someone who is seeking to be forgiven and to forgive yourself for actions you have committed and now deeply regret. You may have a strong Christian faith, be struggling to hang on to your faith or have no faith in God at all. Whoever you are and whatever your reason, this book is for you.

Forgiveness addresses issues at the very heart of human nature and is therefore crucially important and relevant for everyone, whatever their belief. Forgiveness is also very tough. It is not for the faint-hearted, yet is vital for our wellbeing and growth. It's not the natural response to injury and abuse but, on more than one occasion in His teaching, Jesus emphasised how important it is to God that we have a forgiving attitude towards others. Which is why this book will be based on what Jesus teaches on this vital subject, however challenging it may be. We'll consider Jesus' own words and example below as a place to start.

But before we begin, you may be thinking, 'Why is forgiveness so important? And how does it relate to the wrongs done to me or the wrongs I have done?' This book has been written to help you unpack some of the answers to these important questions.

Is forgiveness possible?

Mel Gibson's *The Passion of the Christ* brings to life vividly these words of Jesus on the cross which are the ultimate expression of forgiveness: 'Father, forgive them, for they do not know what they are doing' (Luke 23:34). Jesus forgives the very people who are crucifying Him. And, He is saying to us, 'I am setting you an example of how to forgive the very worst sins.' This is an example of 'tough' forgiveness.

Forgiveness in the face of overwhelming tragedy was also seen recently in the experience of Robin Oake. While Robin was Chief Constable of the Isle of Man Constabulary, his son Stephen (a Special Branch Officer) was killed in the line of duty. A press conference was called, and a journalist asked Robin what he thought about the man who had killed his son. Robin, a Christian, told the journalist that he forgave the man – and his statement was greeted with sheer disbelief and amazement. In his moving and helpful book, *Father, Forgive*, Robin gives gentle advice on the 'hows' and 'whys' of forgiveness with the authority of someone who has truly 'been there'. [1]

Someone else who exemplified the power of forgiveness is Corrie Ten Boom, a Dutch woman who, together with her sister Betsie, was imprisoned during the Second World War for helping Jews to escape from the German-occupied Netherlands. When preaching in Germany after the war, Corrie met one of the guards who had been at Ravensbruck, the Nazi concentration camp where her beloved sister had died. The former guard asked her, 'Will you forgive me?' He was standing in front of her, his hand outstretched, and she was faced with an enormous dilemma: Would she act like Jesus or remain bitter, holding a grudge? It is impossible to imagine her emotions and the memories of brutality and death that would have flooded her being in those moments of decision. She recalls the torment she found herself in:

> I, who had spoken so glibly of forgiveness... could not forgive... But forgiveness is not an emotion – I knew that too. Forgiveness is an act of the will... 'Jesus, help me!' I prayed silently. 'I can lift my hand. I can do that much. You supply the feeling.'... And then this healing warmth seemed to flood my whole being, bringing tears to my eyes. 'I forgive you, brother!' I cried. 'With all my heart.' [2]

The two faces of forgiveness

Before even thinking about how it is possible for anyone to be able to forgive the enormity of the offences committed against themselves or the ones they love, we need firstly to look at the starting point for us all – that of knowing that we ourselves are truly forgiven. People who are 'never wrong' will find it hard to forgive others who wrong them. On the other hand, those of us who have been forgiven by someone else or who know God has forgiven us, will be in a stronger position to consider forgiving someone who offends or abuses us.

During Ron's counselling practice and pastoral ministry, there have been a number of occasions when people have dealt with the issue of being forgiven. Their emotions and personality have been impacted and their whole way of functioning improved. Ron relates:

I remember reading some fascinating statistics: a man who was researching mental illness and hospitalisation stated that if hospital patients could know that they were truly forgiven of their past actions, many of them could be released. What was putting them in hospital, making them physically and psychologically ill, was a lack of assurance of forgiveness. Guilt is a powerful thing.

It doesn't matter whether we are guilty or not; if we *feel* guilty, we act guilty. And that causes huge problems in our lives.

Freely forgiven!

Every one of us has failed in our attitudes and actions towards God. He could have destroyed us but instead He has chosen to offer unconditional pardon – we simply need to receive it. This is an essential foundation for inner freedom. So what really matters to us first of all is our own personal forgiveness. How does the forgiveness of the cross flow to us? When God sent His only Son, Jesus, to die on the cross for our wrong thoughts and actions so that we could be reconciled to God, it was His one-way decision. His forgiveness was there before we responded – for there was a time in each of our lives when we didn't know we needed forgiving. You may be in that place as you are reading these words. As we accept God's forgiveness which has been provided because Jesus took the punishment we deserved, God says, 'I declare you not guilty' and He does this for every person who follows Him. Price paid, new start, clean slate, start all over again. On our part, however, there does need to be a response to His generous offer. But more of that later.

So when Jesus says from the cross, 'Father, forgive them', He *means* forgive them. He doesn't mean, 'Father, wait until they work out how bad they've been, and *then* forgive them!' His enemies didn't deserve it. They were still spitting and mocking and gambling for His clothes. Even this worst of all actions is not beyond God's power to forgive. What an incredible statement. What an amazing God. And once we have experienced this astonishing love and forgiveness for ourselves, this same amazing God will help us to take the first step in our own journey towards greater freedom and personal wholeness through forgiveness – however difficult and painful it might be.

Forgiving others

Just as it's true that living without the knowledge of being forgiven can cause mental and physical suffering and illness, so it is also true that harbouring unforgiveness and bitterness towards those who have hurt us is also very detrimental to our own health and wellbeing.

There's real power in forgiveness and it's a principle God honours. Once, while Ron was pastoring a church, a social worker brought Maria to see him. Maria had suffered with severe depression for many years. Ron recalls:

Her family background was absolutely horrendous. She'd suffered the absolute horrors of life. And so I thought, 'Lady, you are still alive. That's amazing!' As I listened to her story, I told her, 'You have done extremely well', because I wanted her to hear that. I then said, 'The people who abused you have all died so they aren't doing anything to you now. The trouble is, you are still living under the horror of what they have done to you in the past. God says that if we forgive, there can be healing.' Maria replied, 'I can never forgive them.' We talked about the whole issue of forgiveness. But she said, 'I can't do that.' 'I totally understand, I'm not sure I could either, but that's the way to freedom,' I told her. The next day she rang me: 'I've done it!' 'Done what?' I asked. 'I've forgiven each of them,' she replied. I thought to myself, 'How on earth did you do that?' 'Things have changed,' she continued. 'Something lifted off me when I forgave. Something lifted. I felt it go.'

I saw Maria a few months later. Her face was lighter. She explained that she was now able to do things she'd not been able to do easily for years. She'd been able to reduce her medication for depression. Something had changed; some release had occurred within her. It was clearly connected to forgiveness.

Maria did not acknowledge any active faith in God. But, even so, she had followed godly principles and God had operated. Isn't that fascinating?

So this is what it means to say that forgiveness has real power. The problem is in applying it to our own lives. That's when we can really begin to see the healing ministry of forgiveness at work. This is hard enough to do with God's help. It's even tougher in our own strength.

Maria's story raises two other important issues that affect our ability to forgive:

1. Not all offences are equal

Stephen Cherry, in *Healing Agony: Re-Imagining Forgiveness*[3] suggests there are four levels of harm and forgiveness will vary accordingly:

a. Trivial (for example, someone bumps into you in a shop)
b. Serious or real hurt (injustice but with no terrible effects)
c. Significant or painful hurt (injustice with pain and emotional impact)
d. Major unjust harm (traumatic, shattering experiences resulting in psychological/emotional distress)

2. The impact of trauma

Trivial experiences are much easier to address. Trauma is a totally different dimension.

As in Maria's experience, trauma has a number of hidden effects. Trauma triggers self-protective responses in the brain. Over time the response can become triggered when there is no real threat. The pain of the trauma has changed brain functioning.

Responses to trauma

FIGHT   **FREEZE**   **FLIGHT**

Often children are unable to fight or flee so they tend to freeze, burying the offences deep inside, enduring abuse until they are old enough to escape. Often the internalised pain will shape their lives for years to come. The same may be true for adults who experience trauma.

There has been much research and discussion available on the internet over recent years concerning the long-term effects of trauma. Vicky Kelly describes how in trauma, the emotional part of the brain hijacks the rational part of the brain.[4] Clearly, until underlying traumatic issues are faced and addressed in a safe way, the individual will not be in a position to consider forgiveness. This is important for friends and pastoral carers to understand.

Activity

If you would find it helpful at this stage to find out more about Jesus' teaching on forgiveness, turn to Appendix 1 at the back of the book. If you are a Christian, you may also want to remind yourself of the enormity of Jesus' love and sacrifice in bringing you forgiveness, by reading an account of the crucifixion, perhaps in a different version of the Bible (eg New King James Version, Amplified, *The Message*), or by watching *The Passion of the Christ* or another film of Jesus' life and death.

Reflection

- Think about why you have been drawn to reading this book. What are the key areas where forgiveness is relevant in your life? What do you hope will be the outcome?
- Have you suffered a particular offence, injury or abuse? Or have you offended, injured or abused others?

You may like to begin your personal journey by making the following prayer your own:

Prayer

Dear God, help me to be honest in looking at issues relating to forgiveness in my life.

Amen.

Notes

1. Robin Oake, *Father, Forgive* (Milton Keynes: Authentic Media, 2008)
2. Corrie Ten Boom with Jamie Buckingham, *Tramp for the Lord* (London: Hodder & Stoughton, 1974) pp56–57
3. Stephen Cherry, *Healing Agony: Re-Imagining Forgiveness* (London: Continuum, 2012)
4. Vicky Kelly, 'The paradox of trauma-informed care', 8 September 2014, youtube.com/watch?v=jFdn9479U3s [Accessed September 2019]

Chapter 2

The significance of forgiveness: Perceptions

Over the next three chapters, we'll be examining the significance of forgiveness. Firstly, we will look at the practicalities relating to forgiveness and why it is so important.

The power of perception

All of us have experienced times when we've been really affected by other people. And we, in turn, have probably hurt others. Sometimes we are aware of it, sometimes not – that's part of life. But we need to realise that our perceptions can be as powerful and debilitating as the emotional and physical damage inflicted upon us. We don't just *experience* an event – whether physical or emotional, something we hear or see – our *perceptions* about it are really important. For instance, imagine walking into a room full of people who know you well. They suddenly stop talking. You could immediately think, 'They were talking about me – it must have been bad!' But they could have been planning a surprise birthday party for you. So, we tend to interpret things that happen to us with a negative slant. We start thinking, evaluating and making decisions about these experiences – and sometimes our reasoning is not accurate.

Of course some evaluations are 100 per cent accurate. A person (we'll call him Jon) who entered counselling many years ago had a father who was an adventurer and would carry out potentially dangerous activities. The family was never sure if he would return from them. Jon knew that the father didn't like him, as he would walk past him, totally ignoring him, yet show affection to the other members of his family in saying goodbye. Jon felt very rejected – and that was a 100 per cent accurate perception! His father was clearly avoiding him: he didn't speak to Jon and treated him appallingly – and that was how Jon perceived it. So perception can be accurate – but it *may not* be.

We interpret every offence committed against us in some way. And, as we interpret it, we start thinking: 'What does that mean? What is it saying about me? What is it saying about the other person?' This process is true for any deliberate act against us, whether an act of commitment or an act of withdrawal (*not* doing something, as in Jon's story), which can be just as hurtful. As well as trying to deal with our emotions of hurt, pain, rejection or anger, we find ourselves asking: 'What should I do about this? What's the appropriate response? How should I react?'

In addition, we start to question our own self-worth. This is a really important point, especially if we have experienced hurtful things when we were young. It is then that we form our identity, our perception of who we are. So, we find ourselves wondering what this negative experience implies about us: 'There is a message here about who I am; about my value; about my self-worth; about my security, my identity, my relationships; about who I am as a person.' This message can be highly damaging.

The power of words

Were you bullied at school? Did someone make life tough for you? Perhaps it was physical abuse – or putting you down all the time. (Without being sexist, girls can be especially good at that kind of bullying; some seem to know instinctively the power of exclusion and vicious, well-timed words.) You may have been bullied by a teacher or by one of your brothers or sisters – or you may now be trying to help a child who is currently being bullied. When someone offends us like this, a seed is sown that takes root and grows.

Let's take a typical example. Suppose a gregarious ten-year-old girl is so very capable at sport that she intimidates the boys of her age. Feeling threatened, they verbally belittle her with taunts of: 'You're a tomboy. You're not really a girl at all. You should have been born a boy!' Shattered by these cruel words, the girl vows that she will never go through that experience again. She changes from being an outgoing, active person to an inward-looking, quieter type; she abandons sports altogether, pursuing more creative activities instead.

What happened to that girl can happen to us. It frequently transpires in counselling that a parent has said, 'You are hopeless; you are useless; you are ugly; you'll never amount to anything' – with devastating results. These words become barbs. They stay with us. Somewhere along the line we have to come to the point of knowing what to do about them. But how do we deal with them?

There are two common responses. Firstly, we begin to believe the words and act as though they are true. The negative words start to define our identity. Secondly, we make an inner vow that no one will ever say that to us again, so we change our behaviour in an effort to prevent any repeat.

CHANGING THE MESSAGES

So, as we have said, the influence of significant adults or peers on how we see ourselves in our growing years is profound. Such influencers may include parents, grandparents, siblings, church leaders, schoolteachers or fellow students – in fact, anyone significant to us who spoke powerfully into our lives as we were growing up. Adults who speak negative words to children do not always think of the welfare of the child, but are often thinking of themselves.

Two common negative messages people hear in these growing years are: 'You're not good enough' and 'You're not important enough for me to give you my time – you are a nuisance'. It is worth noting that there is a difference between having our *performance* criticised and being criticised for *who we are*. The former, our attitudes and behaviour, may require changing – though not necessarily. The latter is our individual essence – our personality, our inner being, much of which we cannot change. Seeking advice from a wise friend or confidant can help us discover whether we need to change our actions or simply change our thinking towards a pattern more in line with how God sees us.

When these negative comments take hold and we begin to define our value and life direction by them, they can be a major hindrance to our becoming spiritually and emotionally whole as adults. Most of us, as we grow up, listen to these ingrained messages playing in our heads. We dance to their tunes – unless we challenge and change the music and the message. We need to start changing them. We should start by asking ourselves: 'How does *God* see me? What is my true value? Is my real value based in what my drunken dad used to call me? Or do I respect the valuation of my heavenly Father? What is going to steer my life?'

It is absolutely essential that we *value ourselves as God sees us*. We simply cannot effect a change in our thinking and our behaviour unless we have reached the point of believing God's opinion of us. Only then are we able to say to ourselves, 'God values me. God loves me, unchangingly. When I am at my worst He is at His best towards me.'

Ron remembers clearly feeling very inadequate as a young man in ministry, whose role involved attending national meetings.

I grew up in a working-class area and, because of my new ministry role, I ended up at a meeting in the council chambers of Perth, Western Australia, standing on blue carpet with the deepest pile you ever saw. We were all guests of the city council – and I was feeling so uncomfortable! I stood, holding an orange juice, trying desperately to find someone to talk to so that I didn't look too stupid. I watched another man doing something that made me wince, because I thought, 'That could have been me.' He stood talking, totally unaware that he was slowly pouring his orange juice onto the plush carpet – until the steward came along. 'Thank You, Lord, that it was him and not me,' I muttered to myself. Later I realised that this wasn't really a good prayer. But it expressed how I was feeling because I felt so inadequate in that situation. I had to learn to be me – accent and all! This meant changing the messages in my head.

At times, we all listen to this unhelpful, negative self-talk, which tells us who we are. One of the most important yet difficult things to do is to 'change our self-talk', that is, to challenge and change the negative self-talk, replacing it with thoughts that are more positive, accurate and helpful. We need to see that we are no longer bound by what someone has said or how they valued us. We need to focus on God's view of us and to put His new message in place of the old.

Our response

There's no doubt about it: emotional hurt, embarrassment, anger or shame accompany memories of an event that has caused us pain. Where massive physical abuse has occurred, there may also be actual 'body memories'. The person remembers the event, as though it has been impregnated physically into their body. This can have a huge detrimental and damaging effect.

Ron counselled one lady who had suffered major abuse as a young woman. He asked her what, of all she had suffered (and some of it was truly horrific), had been the worst. She replied, 'The worst was when my dad picked me up and threw me against the wall. When he did that, it felt like he completely rejected me.' That was the message she had received. It wasn't just that she had been thrown – she felt as if she had been thrown *away*, like rubbish. This was her perception – and what she had to deal with. The woman did become totally free – but only after a considerable period of counselling.

The good news is that we can become free and move on from our past. But we can't just throw away the old thought patterns; we have to *replace them*. That's why it's critical that we soak ourselves in Scripture, reading passages such as Psalm 139, Psalm 8, Ephesians 1–3 and Romans 8. Reading 2 Corinthians 3 (especially vv17–18) will also bring hope of continuing growth and improvement:

> And we... are being transformed into his likeness
> with ever-increasing glory, which comes from the
> Lord, who is the Spirit. (2 Cor. 3:18)

We are being transformed into Christ's likeness by the power of the Spirit of God. We don't have to stay in the past; transformation can take place once we understand what God is doing in our lives. Honest, heartfelt prayer is an essential element of this restorative process.

'Who am I? How does God see me?' Read 1 John 4:7–21. These words are so powerful – and yet so easy to read and not actually apply to ourselves!

THE DANGER OF SELF-PROTECTION

When our perceptions are firmly in place and those perceptions are faulty, we may feel emotions such as anger and shame. We draw conclusions such as: 'This is who I am. This is how life works for me.' After an emotionally painful experience we may say, 'I don't want to go through that experience again so I'll avoid those situations or those people. I will not put myself at risk again.' People may spend much of their lives trying to ensure they don't get hurt again. But when they do that they are living in the power of the offender, not living free. They may also find themselves living in anger, bitterness and resentment, sometimes for decades.

Certain things that have happened to us were unavoidable – because they took place while we were children. Children are often captive to the pain caused intentionally or accidentally by others – they can't escape it, and that's tragic. As adults, we can evaluate what happened when we were very young, and we add to the thought mix what's happening in our lives today.

Consequently, we may have grown up to be self-protective. We may have formed a faulty picture of ourselves because of what others have said. In other words, we may be bound by our memories of what other people have said or done to us. We begin with an evaluation of what has happened to us and, before we know it, that evaluation has affected our whole lives.

How do we move on from these things?

GENERALISING AND THE WORK OF THE ENEMY

Another problem may arise from our being hurt – we take a specific event and generalise it: 'This person doesn't like me. I am just one of those people that nobody likes!' We make generalisations much more often than we would believe: 'When I tried that, it didn't work – so I won't try anything difficult again.' 'I tried to be friends with that person; they didn't want to be my friend. Maybe nobody wants to be my friend.' Our enemy, the devil, loves this because he's made deception and distortion of truth his primary strategy against humanity right from the start, in the Garden of Eden. We can see from Genesis 3 that Satan succeeds in causing a broken relationship with God, and with other people. He delights in causing division.

One of the biggest things about suffering physical and emotional damage is that it's a very lonely experience. Even if others have been through experiences similar to our own, we feel totally alone; it feels like the universe has suddenly changed and become a lonely, depressing or fearful place. The negative mind messages begin to take shape.

Sometimes our response to things that happen to us makes us tough and unapproachable. We can see that this is the enemy's purpose, for it prevents us developing positive feelings for other people – which is only possible if we allow ourselves to be vulnerable. This seems to permeate all our relationships. If we fall out with someone at church, we start to look around and say of others, 'I wonder when *they'll* fall out with me.' We are generalising the whole process – and then we may become defensive: 'I'm upset about that. It could happen again so I'd better stay a little bit distant from everyone.' And so we begin to withdraw.

The danger is this: we withdraw from people most when we actually need people most. When we do this, we feel completely on our own. When people stop coming to church or house group, or don't visit, we say, 'What's happened to so-and-so?' They may be sick; but it could also be that they are struggling with something that's been done to them – even an imagined offence. Imagined offences are just as painful as real offences – because we have evaluated the offence to mean something it actually doesn't.

PERFECTIONISM
It would be very helpful in this defensive/withdrawing situation if we could learn to laugh at our own failures and to 'lighten up' a little. We shouldn't expect perfection in ourselves or in others – either in church or elsewhere. We're all human!

Activity

How do you decide your true value? By something someone has said, a negative word? Or do you see yourself as God sees you, as described in the Bible? Respect the valuation of your heavenly Father. Let His opinion steer your life. Determine to value yourself as God sees you. Decorate a piece of card or copy the following onto a Post-it note and place it where you will see it often:

'God values me. God loves me, unchangingly. When I am at my worst He is at His best towards me.'

(You could use these words as a screensaver or place them next to a photograph of yourself.)

Reflection

- Do you have an unhelpful thought pattern playing in the back of your mind? Spend time reflecting on the Bible verses mentioned earlier in this chapter. It is particularly helpful to read Psalm 139 in a 'personal' way, as if God were speaking to you: 'I have searched you and I know you. I know when you sit and when you rise...'

- Have you allowed yourself to become isolated or alienated from your family, friends or church fellowship because of something that was said or has happened to you? Bring the offence/offender to God and ask His Spirit to show you where you need to make changes in your thinking and your actions.

- Remember, if you have a Christian faith you will be getting to know Jesus during your times alone with the Lord. As Christians, we grow as disciples in the way we relate to others, overcoming obstacles and difficulties in relationships. Permit yourself to laugh at your own failings and to lower your expectations of the standard of others' behaviour towards you.

Prayer

Loving heavenly Father, thank You that You have the power to change our innermost thoughts, as we invite You to do so. Help me to see today how much You value me, and to let Your evaluation of who I am and what I am worth shape my thoughts and actions. Thank You, Lord.
Amen.

Chapter 3

The significance of forgiveness:
Dumping the sack

Forgiveness is vital. Why? Let us try to imagine offences committed against us as a weight we carry. We don't come out of an experience where someone has offended, hurt or abused us without feeling that we are carrying a sack full of negativity – which may be affecting our thought life.

What does forgiveness do? It releases us, the wounded party, from carrying this negative load. Both a spiritual and a psychological principle are in operation here. When we struggle with the issue of forgiveness, as we all do at times, it becomes a burden; it provokes a mental and emotional struggle: 'What does this mean? What can I do? Will I forgive? How do I do that?'

Upon reaching a point of decision and acting upon it we experience a release. The same principle operates in other areas of life as well. For example, we may be trying to work out whether or not to move house. When we make the final decision, it's a great relief: 'At last, I've done it!' It's very similar to our idea of dumping a heavy load. We say to ourselves: 'I'm not going to carry that weighty sack any more.'

Issues of revenge

Revenge (or thoughts of revenge), on the other hand, does not address the original offence.

Ron remembers watching a snippet of a film many years ago. A man holding a smoking gun is standing in a poorly-lit park. He's just shot his enemy (whom, Ron presumed, he'd been chasing throughout the film) and he asks, 'Why don't I feel any better?' And that was the end of the film. This question perfectly illustrates our point: revenge simply does not address the original offence; it neither changes it nor gets rid of it. It is important to understand this point.

We all meet people who say, 'If only I could go up and hit him/her, I would feel better.' Not true! These injured people wouldn't feel better, they would feel worse – because now they would end up carrying their own offence as well as the original offence done to them. The desire for revenge is understandable, but it never wipes out what was originally done. It is simply not the answer.

Any of us who have tried to take revenge will know that it just doesn't work. We might feel better for a millisecond, but then the other person will want to get even too – so nothing is solved. Such thoughts and actions simply complicate things further for us. There are glaring examples of this occurring on a grand scale between nations, religions and ethnic groups.

Think for a moment about what we see on television: on news programmes or reality shows. Neighbours actually throw things at each other because twenty-five years ago one of them dumped their rubbish too close to the fence. People have been known to end up in jail or even to die because a trivial offence has escalated out of control. Taking revenge simply does not solve anything.

Attitudes and circumstances

Another unsatisfactory response to being hurt is to attempt to make the offender feel guilty or sorry for what they have done. What we are really saying to that person is: 'You have to understand how bad I felt because of what you did to me.' Doing this still binds us to them, while we wait for their repentance. We must reach the point where we see that they may *never* understand. The offender may never appreciate what we felt, no matter how much we tell them, because their temperament and point of view are entirely different to ours. In fact, they may say, 'What are you getting upset about? It was nothing.' This response, of course, just makes it worse because we think that they are not treating the offence seriously. The important fact is that the person who has offended us must come to any sense of regret *themselves*. We can tell them we are hurt, but we can't get them to *feel* what we are feeling. If God shows them, they will know. It usually doesn't work if *we* try to do so.

It's important to realise that sometimes we will have to let the issue go. Talking about the offence won't do any good – although there may come a time in the future when the issue can be raised. Letting go will be necessary in order to move ahead in an ongoing relationship with the person who has offended us. One day it may be appropriate to say, 'We seem to have been having a bad time lately. I think things are getting better, but can we talk about what happened? When you said... I was quite upset. I didn't understand what was behind it.' By saying this we are owning our own 'stuff' (emotions, feelings, reactions, responses) and are willing to hear the other point of view. But we do have to be careful how we phrase our comments.

It is also true that when dealing with ongoing offences, perhaps within a close relationship, it is never good to generalise. Married couples often do this, making statements such as: 'You always…' 'You never…'. These generalisations do not help. The statement: 'You never bring me flowers' could well be true, but to say 'You are always angry' is generalising. It is far better to be specific. For example, by saying, 'Every day for the past two weeks you have been angry when you arrive home from work,' the offending party is given a realistic description of exactly what they have done to upset the other person. If they are told: 'You are basically just an angry person', what can they do about it? They might reply, 'That's your picture, not mine. I think I'm just being reasonable!'

GO PUNCH IT!

Some counsellors make use of large smiling, rocking clowns (air bags with a huge base). They tell the injured party to 'Go punch it!' – but doing so doesn't actually deal with the initial offence. The person punching the clown may well feel better for a while because punching it is helping them to release pent-up emotions, but this doesn't usually lead to a solution of the original problem – unless it surfaces in the process.

However, here is an example of where this approach proved beneficial:

> On one occasion a young woman in her mid-twenties came for counselling. Serena was extremely angry with her father. I said, 'Just imagine your dad's sitting here. He's tied up and can't move his hands and feet, and there's a gag around his mouth… what would you say to him?'
>
> Within three minutes she was absolutely screaming at him! There was nobody there, but she was seeing her

father in that chair. Then she sat back and said, 'I feel
better now.' I asked, 'What do you really want to say to
him now?' She replied, 'I want to tell him how much I love
him, especially when he's not around.' So I asked, 'Would
it help to write down everything you felt then – all the
anger and rejection, whatever it was. Write it out so that
you can actually *see* it. Read it, say it, then tear it up
and write what you want to say to Dad now.' I only saw
her once. Later she phoned and said, 'Things with Dad
are so good!'

That doesn't happen very often – perhaps in one case out of
a hundred. But for this woman, that was it. She didn't act out
her emotions to her father because she didn't feel free to do
so (it probably would have made the situation worse), but she
did express her feelings in a safe way, then evaluated their
cause and decided on a positive way ahead to achieve what she
really wanted.

Whilst we can see that there might be some benefit in the
'Go punch it' technique after all, what was helpful in the above
case was that the young woman actually owned the anger, the
shame, the guilt and the revenge. Owning the offence and the
emotions attached to it by *doing* something is good, but not
enough. There needs to be some way of reaching the next
step – that's extremely important. The offence needs to be
released – we need to 'put the sack down'. Going for a physically
demanding walk or run, or simply taking some time out on our
own when we feel angry, can provide helpful temporary relief.
But in order to gain internal freedom from the offence and the
offender the underlying issue has to be addressed.

What do we do when the person who has offended us,

perhaps a parent or grandparent, is no longer alive? We have reached the point of confessing that what they said or did constituted a major hurt or offence. We are 'owning our own stuff', but it's now impossible talk to the offender about that pain.

The 'shouting at the chair' technique may occasionally be helpful here. It might also be useful to have someone else with us when we reach the point of being willing and able to confess our pain and our reactions to the hurt we have suffered. There is something powerful in hearing our own words speaking out the reality of our experiences, blowing the cover off the confusion and emotions that have been hidden inside. We may need someone to pray with us. The emotions we can feel may be fairly intense. If someone is with us, they can reflect back to us what we have said, both in its volume and intensity. They may also pick up on other things we have not noticed ourselves: for example, how many times we said we were angry or how often we declared, 'You never loved me!'

Confession and ownership

You will have realised by now the importance of ownership; of 'speaking it out'. There is real power in our words. The Word of God created the universe; created us. Think about this. Words are only sounds; just air going over vocal cords. And yet, words are powerful both in causing damage (see James 3:9–10), and also in confession and in healing. Don't just think of confession in terms of saying words such as 'I've done wrong'. Confession also means *owning* what is true. For example, saying 'I was deeply wounded by what happened here' is confession. It's agreeing with God about the truth of the situation; it is stating something that is a fact for us.

It's *communication* that can offend; or the *lack* of it – either positive verbal or nonverbal communication. This includes communication expressed through body language, facial expressions or physical withdrawal – distance. Rejection can be combined with silence or negative words – this triggers the damage. So it is the negative communication that does the harm: the tone of voice, the expression, the message we pick up.

Moving on

Physical assault is a powerful message. Whether it's sexual or nonsexual, it is always experienced and interpreted as negative, painful and damaging. The experience communicates something to us and we begin to interpret it and respond to it in ways we have already discussed. We become bound to and shaped by these experiences, unless we become proactive. A real-life example illustrates this point:

> On discovering that one of her peers had been sexually abused, a teenage girl approached the school counsellor and said, 'I'll speak to her. I've been there, and I have come through it.' Considering the way she appeared in the school, the counsellor was both surprised at her mature and well-balanced approach to her past and pleased that she was feeling whole enough to help another person who was struggling with this monumental issue.

The final result of confession, ownership and ultimately moving on, may not be immediate, but there should be a positive, healthy disengagement – as opposed to harmful attachment to the offender or offence. For many people, it will not be possible to be close friends again with the offender. Forgiveness is not the same as reconciliation, and re-establishing trust is a further huge step. Some people may have to stay away from the person who committed the offence towards them. There may have been an unhealthy co-dependency operating between them, and sometimes the way to re-establish themselves and the relationship is by pulling back a little from the other person. This is not because the injured person is still carrying the offence, but because they realise that what caused the offence was unhealthy in the first place. The relationship has to change in some way. In cases of serious emotional, physical or sexual abuse, forgiveness may be appropriate but rebuilding the relationship may be unwise, even unsafe.

However, it is not always possible to disengage with someone who has hurt us but is still present in our lives – and may still be offending. This is especially true if it is a family member. Whilst an adult may be able to leave the situation, it is much more difficult for children who are caught in the circumstances, with no power or control. Frequently, when they grow up, these children begin to define themselves on the basis of their childhood experiences. So it's crucial that they reach the point of starting to live out of who they are from God's perspective – and not out of how others have defined them.

Practically speaking, in circumstances where we are unable to avoid the offender (especially when they are a family member), and particularly if the offender is a parent, spouse or partner, we have to work hard on setting safe boundaries in place for ourselves. Cloud and Townsend[1] have written and produced an excellent range of books and DVDs on the topic of boundaries, which will help anyone who is facing boundary issues. James Dobson's book *Love Must Be Tough*[2] may be helpful for anyone struggling with knowing how to deal with their spouse's infidelity.

Whatever has been the nature and severity of the emotional and physical damage inflicted upon us, forgiveness is so counter-cultural and so counter-intuitive that it flies in the face of every natural instinct. Only through the empowering grace of God can the power of forgiveness be released in such a manner as to open the way for our personal inner healing and transformation; providing us with the freedom and the new start for which we so desperately long.

Jesus is our example and the Holy Spirit provides the supernatural power of forgiveness.

Forgiveness in marriage

If we are still living in the difficult situation, we must make sure that we don't define ourselves by the offence or the offender. If someone is continually hurting us, for example, in a marriage which has been really dysfunctional, how do we manage to live in forgiveness? Do we have to leave the marriage (or relationship)? In ongoing abusive situations this has to be considered as a matter of safety for ourselves and others under our care.

We can deal with the smaller issues needing forgiveness within marriage in the way we have discussed earlier in this chapter. Instead of making generalisations and saying, 'You always...' we can learn to say instead, 'When you say/do... this is how I feel. I want to withdraw and I feel hurt.' Instead of throwing blame, we are owning our response; we are actually 'owning our own stuff'. This is a positive approach. However, in some marriages, a point may be reached where the marriage is simply not going to work – even with counselling or talking to someone we trust. In a marriage where one person is constantly abusing the other person a functional biblical marriage no longer exists. The degree of the abuse is crucial here. For instance, one lady was regularly being beaten up by her husband, a church elder. Her church had strong, dominant, male leadership; her husband was the head of the family and, according to her understanding of her church's teaching, she just had to put up with it. It took a very long time for her to be able to say, 'I can't stay. I think my kids are at risk of being seriously harmed by their dad.'

But what if the marriage is permitting another sort of harm – that of verbal hurt, criticism and belittling? What if a spouse is being forced in one way or another to do things they doesn't want to do; in effect, emotional blackmail? What if there is serial unfaithfulness? Is there no 'way out' of such misery?

We may know people who have used the verses in Matthew 18:15–17 purely to force someone to leave the church; neither love nor forgiveness has been shown. Rather, it's been a case of their saying: 'I'm right and they're wrong. They're out!' Is this really what Jesus intended here? In the same way, when we think of abusive marriage situations, do we really believe that God intends a person to stay where they might be seriously damaged psychologically and/or physically – or even killed?

Some women have been abused in the name of male leadership in the home; in a Christian context. Yes, the New Testament is sometimes twisted to allow the abuse of women.[3] And, of course, many people feel guilty at the thought of leaving their spouse, whatever the provocation. Christian or not, they simply 'love too much'[4] or are too afraid to leave: afraid of what the spouse might do, afraid of what will happen to their children, afraid of financial implications... and Christian women may also be afraid of what their church (and God) might think. They want to do the right thing; they don't see that often they are being 'battered' into submission.

There are times when, although there is forgiveness, it is simply not safe to stay in the relationship. It may be for a season, but one or other of the partners may have to move out. The authors are not advocating marriage break-up, but marriage should not be used as a way of battering each other. At that point it's not a marriage. The marriage certificate is still legally signed, but the marriage is no longer operating in the way that God intended. Ephesians 5 says that marriage is meant to represent Christ's relationship with the Church (see vv22–33). Is an abusive marriage doing that?

Some of us have grown up in a culture that says divorce is never right; but we are fallible human beings and, for safety's sake, it may have to happen. Jesus taught that Moses permitted divorce because of the hardness of people's hearts. At the same time, He made it clear that this was never God's original plan (Matt. 19:3–9). Sometimes we Christians have a higher tolerance of abuse to ourselves than we should have. We need to start recognising that fact and being honest about how someone has treated us – and how we have allowed it to happen. In a marriage we can operate out of an identity that has been imposed upon us by the other person – rather than recognising that we have our own identity as an individual, as well as our identity together as a married couple before God.

'Let go of the sack'

As we discussed earlier, revenge doesn't work, nor does trying to make the offender feel guilty for what they have done. Sometimes, however, we may reach the point of sharing our feelings in a reasonable way and there may be some understanding from the offender. When, for whatever reason, we cannot get to the place of sharing our pain with our offender, off-loading it to a trusted person may help – as long as we are in the process of 'owning our own stuff'. The reason for this is that in every personally damaging situation, we are likely to have an unhealthy response, which adds to the problem. Confessing what's happened, aligning it with the truth and speaking it out are all good; but we have to take the next step and let it go. 'Let go of the sack.'

When we come to a point of forgiveness we take control of that area of our lives again so that we can make godly choices regarding our future. By forgiveness we mean here: giving up the impossibility of changing the past; owning our hurt, damage and pain; letting go of any desire for revenge towards our offender; and, as far as possible, seeking to move on. We take the power out of the hands of others. Although it may not look like it, when we forgive we are actually saying:

> I am now taking control of my life. The only way I can be free of this offence is to say: 'Move on.' Revenge will get me nowhere. Thinking about it all the time doesn't help. I have come to the point of saying, 'God, if you can forgive me, You can help me to forgive this person.'

We must understand that reaching this point will be harder for some than for others. For some injured people it's not simply a matter of saying, 'Oh well, I'll do it right now!' It may require a journey of months or even years before they reach the point where they are able to say, 'I know I'm ready now. It's daunting, but I know that I have to forgive X, Y or Z.' Additionally, some of us may still find ourselves living with the offender and having to deal with this on a daily basis.

Complicating factors

It is important to realise that a number of complicating factors may make offering forgiveness more difficult – or even unreachable. (This issue is discussed very fully and movingly in Simon Wiesenthal's book, *The Sunflower.*[5]) Each factor on its own will make forgiveness more challenging and more emotionally draining. Some factors are clearly more daunting than others. However, when a combination of these factors is complicating the offence, forgiveness may appear to be a challenge too great.

Complicating factors include such things as:

- when the offender is a family member or close friend
- when the offence has caused major ongoing emotional trauma
- when the offence occurred over an extended period of time
- when there were multiple occurrences of the same or similar offences over an extended period of time
- when the offence has caused permanent physical injury or disability
- when the victim's character and reputation have been permanently tarnished
- when other relationships have been seriously and irrevocably damaged as a consequence of the offence
- when other traumatic or challenging life issues happened at the same time as the offence
- when other persons, who are significant or special to the offended individual, have placed the blame on the offended individual for what has occurred

- when the offended person believes that others who should have protected them when the offence happened have let them down
- when the offence has greatly diminished and undermined the offended person's self-perception and self-belief to the point where they no longer function well in everyday life
- when the offender has died
- when the offended person is overwhelmed with anger or thoughts of revenge
- when well-meaning people urge the offended person to begin to forgive immediately, before they are able to process their pain and have reached the decision to forgive by themselves.

It's not hard to understand how a combination of these factors would build up a wall that becomes an unhelpful defence against forgiveness. It's also easy to see why it's difficult for someone to forgive when their life has been permanently damaged by the offence or offences perpetrated against them.

However, the action of forgiveness sets us free from the offender by overcoming the offence rather than living under it – even when our life circumstances have been permanently changed by it. All victims live under the offence, defined by and bound by it; suffering under the load. We can 'dump the heavy sack', but the fact is that we can be left with scars... We'll look at this in the next chapter.

Activity

Carrying around unforgiveness is like carrying a sack full of negative junk. This practical exercise may help. Collect together a number of large and small stones. Imagine any offences you find hard to forgive as these stones – some bigger and heavier than others. Take the stones into your hands and feel the weight. Then imagine yourself dropping these different stones into a bag, held out to you by Jesus. He invites you to let Him carry the load. Can you do it? And how do you feel, once you have dropped those weights into the bag?

Reflection

- In her book *Broken Wings,*[6] Sheree Osborne tells of an elderly woman who had been abused as a child and had not dared to let anyone into her life since – 'Her life stopped at the age of eleven'. How tragic; unforgiveness can stop us moving on, to the point where we don't really live at all. Think about the fact that revenge, or thoughts of revenge, do not address the original offence. They are only hurting you.
- Your issues of forgiveness may be related to your marriage. Reflect on what you have read above, and seek help and counselling if you feel it is appropriate.
- Think about confession and ownership. Are you able to confess and own what has happened to you and your own feelings about it? Are you able to say, 'I am now taking control of my life. The only way I can be free of this thing is to say, "Move on". Revenge will get me nowhere. Thinking about it all the time doesn't help. I have come to the point of saying, "God, if You can forgive me, You can help me to forgive this person."' Confess it. Own it. And move on!

Prayer

Lord, help me to be real before You as I confess and own what has happened to me and my true feelings about it. Thank You that You forgive me and You alone can give me the power to move on – to 'dump the sack'.
Amen.

Notes

1. Henry Cloud and John Townsend, *Boundaries: When to Say Yes, When to Say No, To Take Control of Your Life* (Grand Rapids, Michigan: Zondervan, 1992). See also cloudtownsend.com

2. James Dobson, *Love Must Be Tough* (Waco, Texas: Word, 1983)

3. James and Phyllis Alsdurf, *Battered into Submission: The Tragedy of Wife Abuse in the Christian Home (Godalming: Highland Books, 1990). Some Christians have found this book helpful.*

4. Robin Norwood, *Women Who Love Too Much* (London: Arrow Books Limited, 1986). Again, this book has been helpful to some Christians.

5. Simon Wiesenthal, *The Sunflower: On the Possibilities and Limits of Forgiveness* (Expanded Edition) (New York: Shocken Books, 1997)

6. Sheree Osborne, *Broken Wings* (Milton Keynes: Authentic, 2006) p217

CHAPTER 4

The significance
of forgiveness:
Living with the scars

Forgiveness is a new beginning, offering an opportunity to address our negative thoughts, feelings and attitudes: feelings of insecurity, worthlessness, being damaged or trapped by the offence. It also carries the potential to break a destructive cycle of harm and revenge which, if unbroken, causes a further sense of being trapped, together with all the painful emotions and responses this releases.

In essence, forgiveness draws a line under a negative chapter in the past. Through our forgiveness, we release the offending party from the guilt that's attached to the offence, from our point of view, following the example of both Jesus and the first martyr, Stephen (see Acts 6–7), who offered forgiveness freely to those who persecuted them. But the fact is, offences scar us and we have to learn to live with the scars.

Balls, chains, knives and bombs

When someone offends against us, attached to the offence there seems to be a ball and chain which is clamped to us and we drag it around. Then if someone else offends us, we drag that ball and chain around too. What happened to us seems to become our focus: the offence becomes part of us. However, sometimes the offence feels more like being stabbed in the back. Ron tells this story:

After an exhausting time away, I attended a local pastors' prayer meeting, on an evening when I would much rather have stayed at home. I did not want to pray at that moment. What did my body language say? 'Don't want to be here, don't want to pray.' One pastor there had a very powerful prophetic gift. He looked at me, walked over and said, 'Mmmm! Big knife!' He repeated those words five times! In my ministry post I was getting well and truly knifed by certain people – and God had showed him. It was as if he were removing those emotional knives. Even after prayer I didn't feel totally better straight away, but something began to lift – it was amazing. I almost felt God say, 'I know what happened to you and I am sending someone to bring healing.' That's part of the ministry of friends. When someone has been wounded, friends come along, recognise the big knives and work out how to remove them.

It's vital to realise that if we have been 'knifed in the back', or worse, there will be scar tissue. If we have dragged a ball and chain around for years, there will be scar tissue. We will be sensitive in that area – almost certainly for the rest of our lives. So, if somebody does something similar to us in the future, we will find ourselves thinking, 'Here it comes again.' (See under the heading 'Spirals', in Chapter 6.) Being healed (removing the knives or the ball and chain) doesn't mean that we think, 'Now nothing like this will ever trouble me again.' In fact, we may well encounter similar circumstances again.

For some of us the offence may have created an unexploded bomb of anger. When we see injustice in some other situation, for example on television, we explode, 'How could they allow that to happen?' Our anger is actually nothing to do with what we've just seen; it's connected to the bomb fizzing away inside us, waiting to go off. Here is a good example of this:

> In attempting to counsel a young man who'd been through traumatic events, I found it difficult to conduct a serious conversation. The defence mechanism he used was humour, turning aside every enquiry with a witty remark. Believing that there could be underlying anger issues, while he was talking I drew a volcano with red lava inside on the whiteboard. He looked at the volcano shape I'd drawn. 'That's me!' he said. 'I'm like a volcano.' And he started to talk. Not about him, but about the volcano. His way of covering up his pain and anger was humour and diversion; talking about anything but the topic of the pain he was experiencing.

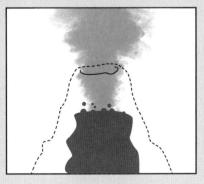

Adults may not respond to something as simple as that, but many of us are very good at turning aside well-meaning attempts to help us address the underlying causes of our pain.

Perhaps we fear that we will not be able to manage the emotions that will surface if we come face to face with our raw, deep-down pain. Or the task may appear impossible.

If the response to our woundedness is anger, then it won't be very difficult for us to get angry again after having forgiven because we've become sensitised in that area; there is scar tissue there. It's vital to be aware of this, but we mustn't judge ourselves too harshly. This is human self-protective behaviour – we don't want to get continually wounded in the same way. But we must be aware that we can react a little too quickly at times.

Anger and blocked goals

Anger is often a signal emotion: a sign that a life goal has been blocked or undermined by someone or something. For example, 'Mike' is a really good football player. He suffers one bad tackle, breaks his leg and can never play again. He becomes very angry at the offender (or at God). Mike's anger is the sign that one of his life goals has been blocked.

If a child is angry, perhaps it is because they are not receiving the love they need or in the way they want; perhaps they feel insecure. Unable to change things or to get what they need, their anger is the indicator; the message that they want things that they aren't old enough or powerful enough to get on their own.

If you are an 'angry type' of responder (one of those unexploded bombs), ask yourself, 'Which of my deep goals was blocked by this particular incident or incidents? What did I want that this experience actually stopped?'

Anger and our attitude to God

There are times when, as adults, we feel anger because we know that we had a right to be loved and secure as a child and that need wasn't met. Frankly, if we don't own our anger, we are in denial. That's why confession is so important: confessing to what *is* – owning the truth of the matter. It's more than the confession of sin, although sometimes that may be involved too. 'God, I deserved a parent who loved me but I didn't get one. I am really upset.' That statement is fine: read the book of Psalms. David was quite willing to express his anger – not just against others, but also against God. 'Where are You? When are You going to show up?' David asks God angrily. And what does God say? 'You'd better put those questions into the book of Psalms.' Think about it. God can handle our anger better than we can, so suppressing it is not the answer. We can say to God, 'I really love You a lot but why on earth did You let that happen to me?' Express your feelings to God.

Some of us grew up in a tradition where we could never say anything nasty to anyone – even if we felt like it. And as for expressing anger to God... we believed that God didn't or couldn't handle anger. But God was angry with Israel; He was righteously angry in Noah's day. God knows what anger is – He made it!

We're not suggesting that it's good to tell God off all the time – that's neither helpful nor healthy. But if we are angry at God we need to say so – He already knows anyway. By being honest with God at such times we may begin to see things from His perspective – and perhaps find the hope He always intended us to have for the future.

Changing our ways of thinking

Cutting off the balls and chains, defusing the bombs and extracting the knives through forgiveness allows us to start changing the way we think and act. But remember: we live in a fallen world, a world very different from the way God wants it. And *we* are not the way God wants us; we are 'works in progress', becoming like Christ as God's Spirit moulds, corrects and shapes us.

As we stated earlier, forgiveness carries within it the potential to break the cycle of harm and revenge. It draws a line in the sand saying, 'That's it. I am not going to be caught in this trap any longer. I'm going to move on – no matter what it costs, no matter how long it takes. This is a turning point in my life.' Our forgiveness releases the offending party from the guilt attached to the offence – from our point of view. When we look at Jesus on the cross and, in response, forgive others, we operate in a way that pleases God and benefits us (Matt. 6:14–15). We are saying, in effect, 'Lord, I have forgiven _____. From my point of view, it's over. I'm not going down that route any longer.' We also have to see that the offender must still carry out their part. If they've done wrong, they need to deal with their 'stuff' (emotions, feelings, reactions and response) before God. But we've let it go.

Forgiveness taps into the raw spiritual power of the heart and will of God because it flies in the face of the worldly response. We could paraphrase Jesus' words like this: 'If you love your friends, who cares? Everybody does that! It's when we love our enemies we know that God's at work' (Matt. 5:43–48). Loving friends is relatively easy… most of the time (although even that can be problematic), but to love our enemies really takes God's help! We can't do it without Him. This, in turn, opens up the chance of a new and more fulfilling future for us – and *maybe* even sometimes for the relationship. If we can't let go of offences, the door is firmly shut. By forgiving, we open that door to new possibilities. Nothing is impossible with God.

Above all things, forgiveness shows recognition of whose opinion counts most: the person who has wounded us, or God whose children we are. Ask yourself: 'Who am I listening to?' Perhaps the difficulty here is that we can't talk to God in the way we can talk to the offender; we can't *see* God or His reaction to us. So we may doubt that He really does see us as the child He loves.

Someone once said: 'Harbouring an unwillingness to forgive is like drinking someone else's poison and expecting that person to die.' Why? Because it kills us. A lack of forgiveness kills us in our spirit and in our personality. What has happened to us will leave scars; but we must learn to deal with them with God's help and through the power of the Holy Spirit. Forgiveness is first and foremost 'a God thing' and He is willing to help us – whether or not we have a strong Christian faith.

A word for friends and pastoral carers

In caring for or supporting someone who has been badly hurt (emotionally, sexually or physically), it's really important to be sensitive. One of the biggest dangers is thinking of forgiveness as a set procedure: 'Do this and that, then it's all gone.' Everybody's journey is different. Every aspect of every type of forgiveness is different. Everyone's right timing to forgive is different, and the way each person processes forgiveness will differ also.

We have to know what God is saying to us; it's really important to consider the timing and the best way to help those we are seeking to support. Why mention timing? While we might agree that forgiveness is the way forward, the timing may not be right as the offended person may firstly need to put other things in place. For example, the individual may not believe that God really loves them. They need to deal with this so that they can begin to change their negative inner thought patterns.

Be aware also that *demanding* forgiveness from the offended person, before he or she has accepted its relevance, may produce further emotional damage. While it's necessary to confront the offended individual with the reality and importance of forgiveness, the timing of actually releasing forgiveness has to belong to the individual concerned. If, as counsellor or carer, we show a lack of sensitivity to their state of readiness, they may feel betrayed by us: withdrawal may follow as a result. They think we just don't understand the level of their pain. We must show empathy. As we have all been hurt in one way or another, we ought to be at least a little understanding when people are struggling to forgive – it's a really difficult thing to do.

Finally, above all else, it's essential that we remain sensitive to the Holy Spirit, His leading and guidance.

Activity

A ball and chain, a knife or a bomb. These are very powerful expressions of hurt. Does an appropriate picture or a representation of the offence in your own life come to mind? If it helps, you may like to draw it.

You may choose to bring your image of damage before the Lord Jesus. As you do so, talk to Him about how the offence makes you feel. He can break the chain, remove the knife and diffuse the bomb. Ask Him to help you deal with the scar tissue. Remember, forgiveness is 'a God thing'.

Reflection

- Do you have any blocked goals in your life? A simple way to know is to imagine yourself going up a flight of stairs and encountering a closed door in the way. What is written on that door? Whose name? Is this where your anger is coming from? Talk to Jesus about it now. Be honest with Him.

- Are you in denial about what has happened to you? Have you pushed it down into the basement of your life and attempted to shut it away? Is this where your anger is coming from? You may need a trusted friend or counsellor to explore what this means for your journey into forgiveness.

- 'Harbouring an unwillingness to forgive is like drinking someone else's poison and expecting that person to die.' Have you been drinking someone else's poison? Is it time to put that cup down, and let it go? If it helps, fill up a glass or cup with water, heavily salted. And, if you are able to let go of the offences at this time, pour it gently down the sink or the toilet, or into the earth. Is there someone you trust sufficiently to stand with you or pray whilst you are carrying out this healing activity?

Prayer

Lord, I praise You that although there may be scar tissue, forgiveness deals with much of the pain. Thank You that You always accept me, love me and are patient with me. Help me to always be honest with You, and to remember that forgiveness is 'a God thing' from start to finish.
Amen.

CHAPTER 5

Seasons of forgiveness:
Steps towards forgiveness

Entering a season of forgiveness

In this chapter we will look at steps we take when we enter a season of forgiveness towards another person.

We have already mentioned that whenever we suffer an emotional or physical wounding, it is a lonely experience – even if people are supporting us. Like a grieving process, the experience is intensely personal. It is especially unhelpful, therefore, for the person supporting or caring to say, 'I know what you're feeling' – whatever their life experience may be. The sentiment is well-meaning, and they may have been through almost identical experiences, but they categorically *do not* know what the sufferer is feeling, because everyone has a different life journey. Every person is different; their painful episode will be unique. Also, each sufferer will reach a season of forgiveness in their own time and way. This is also a very important point. We have to understand that there *are* seasons for forgiveness and they cannot be hurried or rushed. We also must accept that some people may never reach the final point of forgiveness: it may always remain a bridge too far.

1. Know that God is loving

The first and most important thing to do in this whole process is to fix our North Star. In short, it helps when we know how God sees us because it gives us the foundation upon which to move ahead. We must know that God is loving – but what does 'know' actually mean? It's not just knowing the words, it's also *trusting* that God is loving; that He is there and is *for us* not against us; that He understands what has gone on and knows how hard it is for us to forgive; that He Himself is forgiving and is the source and power of forgiveness. *He* is our North Star. We've already mentioned the Psalms: it's worth studying how David dealt with his anger and frustration, giving it all to God.

2. Confession

As we have already seen, confession means agreeing with God who is truth and acknowledging what is true, what is actually going on in our lives – our emotional, spiritual and psychological state. 'What's happening? I'm feeling…, I'm confused, I'm angry, I feel distant from God' – whatever it may be. We need to confess our feelings openly. There's something powerful about hearing ourselves confess (speak out) our struggle with the offence and consequently with forgiving the offender. We are owning up to the fact that what the person has done has impacted us in some way (perhaps dramatically and irreparably); 'ownership' is crucial. Did the offence change our thinking, our lifestyle? What did it do? And then we need to speak out why that impact has made it so difficult to forgive the person who has done it. And remember, God is well able to handle our emotions (however raw and extreme) and our thoughts – no matter what they may be.

Ron tells of a woman who came for counselling:

> In the first session, Janet walked in, introduced herself
> and started talking. I couldn't interrupt her. At the end
> of the session she said, 'Thank you, you were so helpful.'
> I'd just sat there, listening and nodding. I'd barely said a
> word. Janet was hearing her own story – and talking about
> it was bringing the whole thing into a cohesive pattern for
> her. It was probably the first time she had heard herself
> tell the whole story.

So, there is a powerful psychological impact in our speaking out what we feel and think, and what actually happened. Sometimes, while speaking, we suddenly get insights: 'Did I really say that? Am I really feeling that? Is that the effect it's had on my life?' It can encourage us to rethink issues. Although we might do this on our own with God, it's good to have someone with us. The other person can be praying for us or might be able to pose helpful questions. (See Chapter 3, where we touched on this issue when discussing the 'shouting at the chair' scenario.) Listening is hard. Those of us involved in pastoral care or counselling need to listen intently.

3. Choice

We must make clear the fact that a choice to forgive the offender for their offence(s) is required. The wording is important: 'I *choose* to forgive _____ for _____', not 'God, help me to *be willing* to forgive'.

> Michael knew it was time to forgive his father, who had
> died; God had been stirring him. He told me, 'I know
> I've got to do this but I really don't want to. Dad doesn't
> deserve it.' We talked for a while and he said, 'Well, let's

get it over and done with.' Not positive! Michael sat down and was totally unable to speak – not a single word. I suggested, 'Is this the prayer you would need to pray? I choose to forgive Dad for…?' He replied, 'I can't say it.' Michael was stuck. After a while he became really frustrated because he couldn't physically verbalise the words, so he said, 'God, make me willing to forgive.' I told him that was not good enough. He threw something across the room, because he knew it wasn't good enough. He needed to take a step before that – to make a choice. It took another thirty minutes before he could say, 'I choose to forgive Dad.' I watched the tension in him just disappear. He sank down in the chair – absolutely emotionally exhausted.

ISSUES OF TIMING

In the last chapter we discussed timing, but it is worth mentioning again. There is a huge difference between making a decision to forgive (a volitional choice) and feeling 'forced' to do it. To say 'God help me' is in fact an earlier step in the journey of forgiveness: it's a preparatory step because we may need God's help to get us to the point where we are willing to make that choice. And timing is critical. The young man in the scenario above knew the time was right. So, counsellors, beware! To push someone to forgive before they are ready is another form of taking control of the person's life – and is both unhelpful and very unfair. The person needs to know that this is *the* time because God is putting His finger on it.

Even when, as a friend or carer, we observe unhelpful reactions in the victim as a consequence of the offence, these should only be raised after the more urgent issues of owning the pain and releasing forgiveness are dealt with. Otherwise, it's similar to a child being always told to say sorry even when it wasn't their fault; it will just make the person angrier because they feel it is unjust. Forgiveness involves giving up our right to justice and fairness. It cannot be forced. We also must remember that people have very different temperaments: one person might take half an hour to calm down after an argument, whilst another, three days. It is difficult to be clear-headed and objective about the issue of forgiveness when we are still angry.

Certain well-meaning people may have a clearly defined approach to emotional healing. Yet if a sufferer feels compelled to forgive to meet an external agenda and is told, 'All is now well – you can pick up your life again', this 'forced forgiveness' becomes yet another offence added to the initial injustice. It further hinders finding freedom. Remember, too, that it doesn't help to force *ourselves* to forgive before we are ready since, when we find that we can't, we open ourselves up to guilt.

We have to trust God for His timing. Jesus said, 'When [the Holy Spirit] comes, he will convict the world of guilt in regard to sin and righteousness and judgment' (John 16:8). If He can convict the world of such things and we know that He can convict us (He doesn't condemn us – see Romans. 8:1–2 – there's a difference!), then we will trust Him. We can say, 'Lord, I know that I want to do this, but when Your timing's right... Point it out to me then and we'll deal with it together.' In that way we take the pressure off ourselves.

LETTING GO

When my two eldest daughters were quite young and were in the early years of schooling, a violent crime was committed in our area against a young girl of their age. I was not going to let anything happen to my two girls. I used to take them to the bus stop which was only two houses away. Then, in the afternoon, I would say to my wife, 'Don't forget to meet the girls. I don't want them there on their own.'

I was spending time alone with God one night and felt Him say to me, 'What are you doing?' I knew exactly what this was about. I replied, 'I am looking after my girls.' It was as though He then asked me, 'What about at the other end – at school?' Fear started to rise in me and I sat on the floor, my eyes streaming, saying, 'God, I give you my girls. I give them to You individually, whether they live or die, whether they are well or sick, whether they are damaged or not. I trust You with them.' And, with my hands raised, I handed them up to God. It was an act of repentance for me; I needed forgiveness for trying to be God to my girls and I also had to forgive myself. I had to make a decision to surrender my daughters to God. *Could I trust God more than relying on my own efforts*?

This did not mean that my wife and I did not exercise good parental care, but something of the impossible burden of responsibility was lifted off me in that encounter with God. Trusting God to help us with forgiveness is very much like this.

Choosing to forgive, letting go, will bring effective emotional and spiritual release.

4. Freely give

When we offer forgiveness there should be no strings attached. Saying 'I will forgive if (s)he recognises (s)he has done me wrong' won't work. The offender may never do so. We remain chained to the offence because we continue to allow the offender to dictate what happens in our lives.

Jesus encouraged the development of a forgiving spirit (Matt. 18; Luke 17:1–5). This is based upon recognition of human frailty and the importance of the freedom and healing that forgiveness offers to us as much as to the other person; it is not a sign of weakness or naiveté. Forgiveness is hard and is not for the faint-hearted. It takes real courage to forgive somebody, as those of us who have ever reached that point well know. The more intense the offence, the more difficult it becomes.

Greater personal wholeness

Forgiveness releases the potential of greater personal wholeness because the offence will continually block our spiritual and emotional growth. Every time we try to move forward, the offence will become a trap for us. The more offences we have gathered (the greater the number of knives in our back), the more difficult it will be to move on in our life because these knives can always be twisted a little more by someone else. And they will stop us growing in God.

One woman recalls:

> When I was young, I was engaged to be married to the only man I have ever loved. A few months before we were to be married, my sister stole my man and married him. She was not a Christian, but I was. I began to pray that my sister would become a Christian but nothing happened. I

prayed for decades. Then, one morning during a church service, I realised my problem was that I was thinking to myself: 'If my sister becomes a Christian she will realise the incredible sin she has done me by stealing my husband-to-be for herself.' (Source unknown.)

This woman had suddenly realised that her prayer was loaded; her motives impure. She repented before God and moved on. She hadn't dealt with the offence and so it had become a trap in her life.

CRITICAL POINTS

Here are a number of critical points in this process of forgiveness:

1. *Own the pain the problem has caused.* We have already touched on denial. In counselling we find that denial of pain – 'It didn't really touch me or affect me' – is a really difficult issue. Denial will block any release and healing.

2. *Decide to pursue forgiveness* for the offence of another person – even if the offence was not committed directly against us, but against someone we love. This may be very difficult emotionally but we need to reach the point of saying, 'I am going to pursue forgiveness. I want to forgive this person.' This may be very stressful. We may feel that if we connect deeply with our pain it will destroy us, or that if we release our emotions they will erupt and literally kill us. In counselling, this becomes very difficult to address. If the injured person has an intense sense of pain it has to be faced if they are to be free of it.

3. *Verbalise it.* We have already talked about verbalising, 'speaking out', regarding issues of forgiveness. Start pouring out blessing on the offender: 'I forgive _____

Lord, bless them!' Once over that hurdle, it's much easier to pray healing back on ourselves. It's a two-way thing: praying God's blessing on the one who has hurt us, and then asking Him for healing for ourselves, results in the power to move on. The hardest part is choosing to forgive... saying it. But when we do, we can speak freedom to ourselves.

4. *Bring closure.* Deciding to pursue forgiveness for the offence of another person is emotionally difficult, but after we have verbalised it we bring closure: 'Lord, take me past this event. I don't want to go back to it any more.' Of course the circumstances and consequences of the hurt or injury won't have changed; for example, our child, killed by a drunk driver, will still be dead; our husband/wife will still have left us for that other person – but we are not 'going round in circles' any more. We have broken free. We are not constantly looking back, unable to go forward. We are willing to move on. It is as if we have opened a gate and are asking the Lord to shut it behind us. Of course, this does not mean we won't feel times of pain or that our memory will suddenly be erased.

5. *Remind yourself that you* did *forgive.* We must realise that forgiving is not the same as getting rid of the pain. Forgiveness is a choice, but the pain sometimes resurfaces because we meet the person again or find ourselves in another situation where the pain arises. Or there may still be a gaping void in our lives. We may then think, 'Did I really forgive?' Yes! God heard. (It's the same as confessing the same sin. God tells us that He forgives us when we bring it to Him, but we are unsure whether we have been heard or have confessed it in the right way. If we have come to Him in genuine repentance He has forgiven us. See 1 John 1:8–10.)

6. *Work it through.* Finally, we need to affirm and recall what we have said and done, then work out that forgiveness in our lives. We need to define ourselves differently, which means seeing ourselves from God's perspective, as mentioned before.

Both God's timing and His encouragement are critical for the whole issue of forgiveness to be appropriately addressed in our lives. As a friend or counsellor, we may reach the stage where it seems apparent that the person we are supporting is in the right season to forgive. However, they keep on going over and over the offence in their mind, not achieving any kind of resolution. What might we do? We could perhaps address this sensitively by using an example from our own lives, explaining how God helped us through it. But that, of course, may not always be helpful, particularly if we were able to forgive someone who injured us in a particular way and they are still struggling to do so. It might make them feel even worse! We must proceed with caution.

We really must understand that timing will be different for each individual because of the intensity of their suffering. It might be better to say, 'You realise that at some stage you will need to deal with this because you keep going over it and it's not getting you anywhere.' Pointing out a way forward can be helpful.

Constantly going over issues that have been forgiven indicates either:

a)   further attention is needed (because we are trapped in an endless circle) or

b)   we are spiralling our way upwards out of the experience, while still dealing with points of pain.

Many of us have been taught at church that if we keep going over an issue, we haven't forgiven. But, whilst there should be a change in the way we think of the issue after we have released forgiveness, *it doesn't necessarily go away*. We will, however, be able to look at it differently.

In the next chapter, we will explore further the preparation needed when we begin to forgive – and think about what 'from this day forward' really means.

Activity

We have covered a lot of ground in this chapter. Review what you have read and write down what means the most to you. Spend some time with the Lord, contemplating His love for you, the importance of confession and choice, giving freely, and personal wholeness. Are there any issues you haven't quite grasped? You may find it helpful to discuss these with a trusted friend and to pray together.

Try to spend some time in reflection and prayer focused on 1 John chapters 1 and 4.

Reflection

• Do you know and believe that God loves you unconditionally? Do you really believe that He is for you and not against you? If you do, thank Him for His love for you. Thank Him for His good plans for your life. If you find that hard to believe, be honest with Him. Ask Him to pour out His Spirit on your whole life, so that you can take a firm grip of His promises for you and believe in them. Read Isaiah 43:1–5a and know that you are precious and honoured in His sight.

- Are you saying to yourself, 'I must forgive', but you still can't, so you are starting to feel guilty? If this is how you feel, let go of the condemnation. Trust God to move in your heart and life. He knows when you will be ready to really let go and move on.
- Look again at the critical points on pages 68–70. Spend time meditating on them and thinking about what each point means for you.

Prayer

Lord, please give me a real sense of Your wonderful presence as I take the steps needed to be free. I ask You to cleanse my heart and my mind so my prayers will be pure. I trust You to give me the power to choose to forgive, knowing Your perfect timing. I trust You that I will be able to forgive sincerely those who have hurt me – with no strings attached. Thank You for Your presence on my journey.
Amen.

CHAPTER 6

Seasons of forgiveness:
From this day forward...

Preparing to forgive

For some who are confronting this decision to forgive, it will be important to have a trusted friend and confidant to share the journey. If we are going to take the journey on our own, we need to find a safe place where we will not be interrupted; somewhere quiet, where we feel comfortable. Having done that, it is then important to affirm God's perspective of us. This underlies our true identity, our value to God and our future hope. If a friend or counsellor is involved, they might add their own positive perspective too, for example: 'I value your friendship; you are a loving, caring person. I don't believe the negative things said to you – they are untrue. It's not the way I have come to know you.' They can agree with you as to how difficult and hurtful the offence may have been but also encourage you that God can enable you to reach a place of forgiveness and move on to a better future. Of course, in our pain, we might question the very idea that God is good: 'If You're good, why are You letting me go through this? Why did You let it happen? It's going to affect the rest of my life. Why? Why? Why?' We have to get real with God; we may even have to forgive Him for allowing us to go through this. And yet, He tells us He will never leave us or forsake us (Heb. 13:5). Somehow, He's in the middle of the pain with us. Frankly, we may just have to get to the point where we accept that we will never know 'why' – and trust Him anyway. After all, if we turn away from Him, who else would we turn to (John 6:68)?

God loves us. Remember: He is for us not against us. We may sometimes feel that suffering is God's way of removing the 'kinks' from our lives – He lets us be hurt, abused, battered and beaten. That's not right, for that is not His character. He is a God of love. He may allow things to happen but not because He enjoys seeing us being beaten up, literally or otherwise. God does not waste even our most painful experiences for, with our co-operation, He can shape our character and bring us closer to Him through even the most ungodly circumstances (see Romans 8:28; also read the story of Joseph in Genesis 37:1–36; 39:1–50:26).

Occasionally people who have suffered abuse have actually experienced God's love and healing when remembering their trauma. One had a dream:

> In the room [where the abuse had happened] the door was always locked when the offence took place, but in the dream Jesus came and opened the door so there was a way out. I knew there was a way out of this for me.

In another case, someone saw Jesus there weeping. These are two powerful images of how Jesus felt about the situation; in one, He opened the door, a clear message saying, 'You are not caught in this for the rest of your life.' In the other dream, He was distressed by what was going on.

Affirmation

The New Testament is full of affirmations about a God who loves us. It is important to keep this in mind, however hard it is, as we begin to take our practical steps in forgiveness. We must remember the following points – and that God has a view of us that is good.

1. *We are loved.* God loves us!
2. *We are accepted.*
3. *We belong to Him* – we are not lost.
4. *We are valued.* He values us more than sparrows, more than the rest of His earthly creation (see Matt. 10:29–31). We are unique!
5. *We are forgiven.* God has forgiven us (John 3:16; Eph. 1:7–8)
6. *We have a promise of hope and a future* (Jer. 29:11).

Romans 5:1–11 is a most encouraging and helpful piece of Scripture that affirms what God has done and what He is doing now in our lives. Read it through a number of times, replacing 'we' and 'us' with 'I' and 'me' as you read. This may become a very personal and intimate time with God as you enter into the central hope recorded here.

Facing the damage — the cost

We affirm God's view but we must take into account the intense inner conflict we may experience as we face the offence or offences that have so harmed us. Genuine forgiveness is never cheap. It cost Jesus; it costs us. Forgiving may be perceived as losing out twice. There was a loss caused by the offence; somebody took something from us. And then we have to give – forgive; we give up our sense of revenge and of justice. Instead of thinking, 'That person's going to get it. God'll get them – or somebody else will!' we say, 'I give up that right'.

It is a struggle, so as friends and carers coming alongside the offended person we need to ensure we don't take lightly the fact that it *is* a struggle. The wounded party has to be willing to own and to face the damage done. It is important that ownership is specific – actual harmful events, experiences and actions. Generalisations such as 'They hurt me [or my son/daughter] for many years' simply won't be enough. It should be about '*who* did it, *what* they did and *how* it hurt me'. The offended person may find it hard to receive or accept affirmation, or positive and hopeful comments from others. Patience and understanding are an absolute 'must' for those who seek to support them.

It is worth remembering that sometimes it is even more difficult for us to forgive the person who has abused, injured or abandoned someone we love than it may be for the person who was actually abused, injured or abandoned – who may well have forgiven. For instance, a mother might not have forgiven her son-in-law for abandoning her daughter and grandchildren, but the daughter may have a good – if distant – relationship with her ex. A daughter may not forgive her mother for leaving her father, and yet the father might have forgiven and moved on.

The step of owning and facing the damage done may therefore be a major obstacle, especially if the pain was caused by, or to, someone who has been significant in our lives. But when the harm has occurred within a church context, it may be even more complicated. The problem with this sort of damage is that it is done in a place where we believe we should feel safe, and it has been perpetrated by people we believe we should trust. So there is a breach of trust and spiritual complications may also follow. This is really one form of 'spiritual abuse' and is very difficult and painful to deal with. It is also, sadly, very common.

Facing the damage — our reaction

Let us take time here to think about what we have already learned. The importance of ownership, or the nature of what occurred *and* the effect it had on us, cannot be stressed strongly enough – especially as we come to the actual step of forgiving. The injured person needs to say, 'This is what was done to me, Lord. This is how it has impacted on my life and my thinking; this is how it has affected me.' We have to be honest about it; honest with ourselves and honest with God. This is repentance in its wider sense. Repentance is bringing our thinking and behaviour into line with God's perspective – in line with the truth.

Our reaction to bad experiences and our reflection on them confuse and distort both the memory of the experience and our responses to it. When something bad happens, as time goes by we twist it. Our perception, our thinking, our reflection, our other experiences all play a part. So what may have been, in its time, a little offence is now a big offence. Some things that happened to us as children wouldn't worry us at all as adults. But now, as an adult, we look back and feel like that child again, saying things like, 'I could have stopped or avoided it.' In that instance, it's good to find a photo of ourselves at the age when the offence happened and to ask: 'Would I expect a child of that age to do what I have been thinking and saying?' No. We tend to view our childhood experiences from the point of adult thought and feeling.

Sometimes we feel trapped by what happened and hopelessness can rise up. We focus on the offence and offender: 'Why did they do that? What did I do to deserve it?' or 'How could they have done such a thing? What more could I have done to have prevented it?' Unanswerable questions. Mentally reliving the past experience, while trying to change the outcome, can produce only a fruitless cycle of regret: a case of 'If only...'. But we can't change the past. The important thing to do is to ask: 'What am I going to do from now on?' 'Who am I going to be from this point on?' 'How am I going to deal with what has happened and move on?' As we take steps towards forgiveness we find that, with God's help, we are empowering ourselves and pushing ourselves to move forward. That's healthy.

We must recognise that everyone responds differently to hurt, offence, pain and abuse, while accepting the reality of our feeling and thinking – even if it's faulty. It's our reality – and that's what we are dealing with. If our thinking is faulty, acknowledging it is a good start; for example: 'I keep telling myself I am useless, I am ugly, I'll never amount to anything.' In this, we are acknowledging that we are saying the words even though they may not be true. It's a simple change of perspective, but it can help.

Spirals

By now, you'll have realised that forgiveness does not work to any predictable plan or order – '1, 2, 3, forgive'. Some people see forgiveness as a circle: we start at point A and forgive someone; something goes wrong and we're back at point A again. That's incorrect. Forgiveness is a spiral.

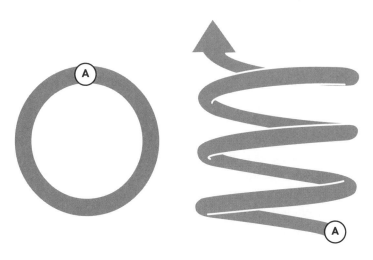

As mentioned before, our scarred areas remain sensitive. When growing in healing after a particularly damaging experience we might be touched with similar pain or damage by another person (or the same one) and we feel the same way as before. We then question whether we have truly forgiven. We did forgive – but now we are learning to live out that forgiveness. As we spiral upwards out of the painful experience and find ourselves in similar circumstances, we must realise that we are *not* in the same situation as before. We have moved onwards and upwards. Thinking in terms of spirals can be very helpful.

Forgiving is an act of will – 'Before God, I choose to forgive.' It's as solid as a marriage commitment or signing a legal contract: Working out the forgiveness is a different matter. When we marry, we may walk back down the aisle feeling no different to when we walked up it. But we *are* different. (See also critical point 5 in the last chapter.)

Not a quick fix

Some people find a sense of release follows immediately after making the choice to forgive. Nevertheless, whatever the immediate outcome, forgiveness should not be viewed as a 'quick fix', even if we do feel the sense of a burden lifting. The damage the offence has caused may require the ongoing gentle working of the Holy Spirit to restore us to wholeness.

Minor offences might be dealt with relatively easily, but for other more serious offences, working out the decision to forgive and letting the healing become a full part of our lives may be a lengthy journey. Often the emotional pain begins to loosen after a period of time, as we continue to embrace forgiving attitudes, but this timescale will vary from person to person. It also depends on the number of similar harmful experiences that come our way throughout life, and whether or not the person who hurt us is still offending. It can't be stressed enough: *we have to remember that there is a difference between mild offences and deep, long-term offences;* forgetting the offence is not always possible – the consequences may remain for life. Forgiveness deals with the guilt of the offender and the control of the offender over our lives. And that is the way to freedom.

Activity

Below are suggested points to help you move into forgiveness and release.

- Are you sure you are a child of God? Be aware that He truly loves you, enough to die for you. He has paid the price of your forgiveness and He is your healer.

- If what you are struggling with has been a major offence, find a safe place, along with a trusted friend, as you begin to forgive.
- Worship God. Ask Him to bring to mind anything that stands between you. Seek His forgiveness for anything the Holy Spirit shows you.
- Wait on God for His insight into what was done to you.
- Invite the Spirit to show you how He wants to release you into forgiveness.
- When the timing is right, and you are acknowledging what was done to you and its effects, you may begin to feel intense emotional pain. Don't allow this to prevent you from moving towards freedom.
- Name before God the offender and the offences and the impact they have had on your life. If possible, speak forgiveness towards the offender, remembering that this is a *choice* not just a desire.
- You may wish to say this prayer: Heavenly Father, I choose to forgive _____ for _____ and I ask You to release him/her from the guilt of what he/she did to me [or to _____ whom I care about]. Please heal me from the effects of that offence on my life. In Jesus' name.
- Don't give in to temptation to water down your prayer (ie 'Lord, help me to forgive' or 'God, I want to forgive...').

_____

Reflection

- When you read through the list above, were you able to apply it to your life at this point? If so, praise God that He has heard you. If not, don't condemn yourself. Ask God to give you a new sense of His perfect timing.

- Take a moment to look at the six points under 'Affirmation' (p75). Which one of these means the most to you right now? Why?
- You must face the fact that there will always be unanswerable questions about the past. The important thing to ask is:
    - What am I going to do from here on?
    - Who am I going to be from this point onwards?

  How we live from this day forward is the important issue. Make sure you fully acknowledge that as you spend time reflecting on this chapter.

Prayer

Lord, thank You that I am loved and accepted. I belong to You and You value me. I am forgiven for You have forgiven me. And I have the promise of a good future. Lord, when I feel I haven't forgiven and yet I know deep down that I have, remind me of the spirals of life and help me to live in the freedom You have bought for me.
Amen.

CHAPTER 7

Forgiveness when *we* are the offending party

The importance of honesty

God is loving, understanding and forgiving. Through Christ's death on the cross, He takes all our sin and wrongdoing, and gives us new life. All this – while we were still ignorant of His love and forgiveness towards us! That's mercy – God's free, unmerited, unearned favour and forgiveness in response to our sins. He knows our hearts. Nothing is hidden from His sight. We all offend – we all need forgiveness. When we offend against another, He knows about it.

It is futile to think that we can change the past. It is also futile to deny that the offence occurred or that it was significant, or to try to water it down by pointing out the failings of others involved. Sadly, there is a tendency in human beings to attempt to justify the most obviously sinful actions. The first step in forgiving ourselves, therefore, has to be acknowledging the offence to ourselves. We must seek and receive the mercy and grace of God. We have to come to God and say, 'You have paid the price of my forgiveness. I throw myself on Your mercy. I have sinned. Please forgive me. Give me the power to overcome this so that I don't go this way again.'

It can be helpful to confess not only before God, but also before a confidential and trusted person, possibly with some counselling or pastoral experience. In doing this, we should be specific and totally honest. James 5:13–20 encourages confession.

1.   Once it is confessed, there can no longer be any pretence that there is no issue.

2.   Confession provides a chance for prayer, support and healing to occur.

As we confess, we must be careful not to blame others. We should confess only our own sin.

Once we have confessed, we must make restitution if that's relevant or possible.

Restitution and reconciliation

Luke 19:1–10 relates a perfect example of what happens when God starts transforming a heart. Zacchaeus, the tax collector, says, 'I have stolen in all sorts of ways but I'm going to give it all back and more.' That's one example of what occurs when our conscience is stirred; we begin to pay back money taken. Companies report that a ballpoint pen may be sent back to them in the post ten years after an employee has left! More seriously, a man might have been pilfering money over a period of years and God convicts him of his sin at the very time his company is downsizing. Should he confess? If he does, he risks being sacked and his whole family will suffer...

In making restitution, we may also have to consider any possible legal implications. If crimes have been committed, the person may have to come before God and seek the wisdom of godly people as to whether any action should be taken.

It's good to actively seek reconciliation (see 2 Cor. 5:16–21) but it may not always be possible. God wants to be reconciled to us and we need to be reconciled to one another. Reconciliation is about restoring relationships. But it's not always wise, and we have to be sure it is the right thing to verbalise it to the other person.

If it is both *possible* and *appropriate*, we should humbly confess and repent before the person we have offended – they need to know we are sorry. But be aware that in some circumstances, this may not be appropriate. For example, the person may not be aware of what we have done. As a rule, it's best to actively seek restitution *if this is in the best interests of the offended party*. In other words, we let the good of the offended person be our guide when seeking to confess to a sin against them. For example, it would almost certainly not be in their best interests to admit that we have secretly hated them for years, but that God has now convicted us of our fault and we're sorry. In a situation like that, the offender might feel released but the offended person would now carry the weight of new and potentially damaging knowledge. In such cases it is usually best to confess the fault to a trusted person and before the Lord – and leave it at that.

If a person comes under personal conviction for an offence against another person, what should they do? Make a face-to-face apology? Send a letter or email? Make a phone call? Do nothing at all? The offender always needs to consider the best interest of the offended person, especially if the offended person is likely to feel unsafe. The offender should always seek objective advice from someone they trust before taking any action.

In cases of serious abuse, reconciliation should not even be considered, even if apologies are offered. Again, the good of the offended person must be the guiding principle.

Reconciliation can never be guaranteed. Even after a relatively minor offence, we run the risk of being rebuffed. We may have gossiped about somebody and they've found out. We confess, 'I'm really sorry. I know I've done the wrong thing. Can we somehow sort this out?' Mortally wounded, they say 'No'. They may never want to sort it out – they have that right.

Even if there is no way to sort out the damaged relationship, we can always pray for the person we have hurt. When restitution and/or reconciliation simply is not possible, we can pray specifically for them, asking God to bless, restore and heal.

Rebuilding trust

We have to rebuild trust where appropriate. One step further than reconciliation, this is much harder. Once trust has been breached, it has to be earned again if it is ever to be restored. Rebuilding broken trust is a process: it takes time. Some people may never feel able to trust us again after the offence, so rebuilding trust isn't always achievable. The same warnings apply here as with reconciliation.

Forgiveness relates to the guilt; reconciliation deals with the relationship. Reconciliation brings the situation back to neutral (if not positive) instead of negative. Restoring trust means being able to walk together in the future. Here, we see three different elements. Forgiveness means that we have resolved the offence and have moved on. Reconciliation relates to the level of restoration of relationship. Trust is a deeper level of healing still. Can the offended person have confidence in the offender again? Can we walk together? Can we work together? Can we have a friendship? Each case will be different.

Trust within marriage

What if there's been a serious breach of trust within a marriage? There's been confession and an attempt at reconciliation; the injured partner has said, 'I forgive you – but I don't trust you.

However, I am willing to walk with you.' In this case, the couple would have to draw boundaries and guidelines so that the offended person could regain the trust that was lost. The issue of trust is largely in the control of the offended person because the offender can no longer set the boundaries where trust will operate.

Unfaithfulness in a marriage is one of the most difficult situations to manage. These are some of the difficult questions that arise, for which there are no easy answers:

- If the spouse is unaware, should the unfaithful partner simply talk in confidence to someone who can hold them accountable for redirecting their focus towards their marriage partner and dealing with any entanglements related to the unfaithfulness?
- What if the affair occurred a decade or more ago and has been over for many years?
- What if there is a real risk that disclosure will end the marriage?
- How will disclosure affect the children of the marriage?

We must add that various conflicting points of view are expressed by mature Christians on this subject. The critical tension points are the desire for transparency yet the risk of destroying the marriage in the process. There are no simple answers.

Forgiving ourselves

When we have done all we can to bring an end to the offence with the person we have hurt, the hardest thing is to forgive ourselves. As a Christian, if we have been convicted by the Spirit of God (if we have been in the wrong), we tend to say, 'How do I forgive myself?' This is an important point.

In 2 Samuel 11–12 we find the famous example of King David's adultery with Bathsheba. She conceives, and the prophet Nathan tells David, 'The child is going to die.' So David fasts for a week but the child dies. By this stage, all the courtiers are thinking: 'The king was in a desperate state when the child was sick. What is he going to be like now that the child is dead?' But David surprises them. He has a wash, changes his clothes, goes to worship God, then has a meal. 'I've done all I can,' he says. 'I prayed for the child's life, but God has taken him – so now I am going to move on.' That's how we must be. It's not easy for us, nor was it for David. His crime was not only adultery, but also murder and deception; it was horrendous because it impacted so many innocent people.

We too may find that we are living with the consequences of our actions for a very long time. But somehow we have to move on in that situation and live humbly as a forgiven person (Rom. 8:1–17), recognising our weak areas and protecting them as far as we can. Then we have to start challenging and changing our unhelpful thinking, establishing new and biblical ways of thinking, behaving and choosing (see Col. 3:1–17) concerning:

- God
- self
- others

This is a deliberate 'moving on', rather than saying, 'I forgive myself' but staying stuck in regrets that disempower us. It is saying, 'Now I'm going to live out my forgiveness.' We have to make a conscious effort. By this, we don't mean that we advocate minimalising what has happened. Instead we embrace the work of the cross of Jesus Christ and apply the forgiveness given to us through Jesus, so that we can continue to be transformed into His likeness (2 Cor. 3:18).

Christian friends

We do need to commit ourselves to Christian friends with whom we feel safe, and who can hold us accountable – not in a controlling way, but by asking us how we are managing in the area of the offence, if it is likely to be an ongoing struggle. We give them permission to speak into our lives. Close friendships provide a natural accountability, not a forced supervision, and within good Christian relationships we can help one another grow in our faith journey. We can also help each other to enjoy God's presence through worship and prayer as a natural part of life, rather than merely relying on formal meetings.

Conclusion

Forgive *and forget* may seem a 'good' idea but, except perhaps in the case of very minor offences, it may be unrealistic. For the most part the painful memories, shrouded and distorted perhaps by time, will live on in our thoughts, our feelings and, in some circumstances, within our bodies. Remember that the wounds Jesus suffered on the cross were still visible after His glorious resurrection. He understands. Nothing can separate us from His love!

Forgiveness is a journey, and often a difficult one, but it is not impossible. It is, however, a necessary journey if we want to enjoy the true freedom that is ours in Christ. Remember, '[God] is faithful and just and will forgive us our sins and purify us from all unrighteousness' (1 John 1:9). We pray that this will be your ongoing experience as you seek to follow and trust in the one who died to forgive us all our sins and to enable us to live in freedom.

Whatever you do, draw closer to God; become more responsive to His warnings and promptings. Invite the Holy Spirit to fill your life and guide your walk. He is the Spirit of truth.

Activity

Read through Psalm 51 in various translations of the Bible – for example, New International Version, New King James Version and *The Message.* Try to get a sense of the power of David's words; they show a heart full of repentance. Affirm out loud that God is faithful and will cleanse us from all our sins as we come to Him in repentance (1 John 1:5–10), that there is no condemnation for those in Christ Jesus (Rom. 8:1), and that He is the one who enables us to live in freedom. Try to write your own psalm, reflecting your feelings.

Reflection

- Confess your sin to God, knowing that He loves you and accepts you. Ask Him for wisdom about the path of restitution (if appropriate), reconciliation and trust. Be sensitive to the Holy Spirit and remember that you are seeking the good of the person you have offended. Pray for them.
- Do you have any really good Christian friends to whom you are happy to be held accountable? If you don't, ask God to show you who He wants to put in that position in your life. If you do, praise God for them.

Prayer

Loving heavenly Father, thank You that you love me, You accept me and You declare that there is no condemnation for those who are in Christ Jesus. You are for me, not against me. Forgive me where I have sinned against others knowingly and unknowingly.

Fill me afresh with Your Holy Spirit so that I can live in His power, knowing His presence as He makes Jesus real to me and helps me to live in a way that is pleasing to Him. [Take some time to find God's peaceful presence.] Thank You, Lord. Amen.

CHAPTER 8

A lifestyle of forgiveness

As we conclude this book it is our hope that you will have been helped and encouraged to release forgiveness to those who have hurt you – and will have found a deeper level of forgiveness and peace in the areas in which you have hurt and offended others.

How then do you live from now on – having understood the importance of forgiveness? How do you live as Jesus teaches us to live: as forgiving and forgiven people, free of bitterness – free to be the people God created us to be? (If you have not yet read Appendix 1, Reflections on Jesus' Teaching on Forgiveness, we recommend you read it now.)

Love your enemies!

Whenever we come to the point of being forgiven, or whenever we bring another person to the point of being forgiven, there is an amazing turnaround. We may not fully understand how it operates, but there is incredible and powerful freedom in this act of forgiving and being forgiven. In Matthew 5:43–48, Jesus told his listeners:

> You have heard that it was said, 'Love your neighbour and hate your enemy.' But I tell you: Love your enemies and pray for those who persecute you, that you may be sons of your Father in heaven. He causes his sun to rise on the evil and the good, and sends

rain on the righteous and the unrighteous. If you love those who love you, what reward will you get? Are not even the tax collectors doing that? And if you greet only your brothers, what are you doing more than others? Do not even pagans do that? Be perfect, therefore, as your heavenly Father is perfect.

'Love your enemies'! We ask, 'Jesus, why do You make it so hard?' We certainly can't love our enemies in our own strength – as we have stated earlier, forgiveness is '*a God thing*' – and we need His help to be able to love and forgive like this. What Jesus is saying is, 'You need a transformed life if you are going to live the message I preach, and this is what living a transformed life looks like. You look at an enemy and say, "I am going to forgive you."'

A man was walking past his timber yard one night and found the gate wide open. There was a lorry in the yard and two men loading *his* timber! He asked them, 'What're you doing?' 'Just loading some timber,' they replied. He responded, 'What are you going to do with it?' And they told him. He said, 'Wrong wood. That's the wood you need, over there.' 'You know we're stealing this timber and you're helping us?' they asked, incredulously. He told them, 'I'm not helping you. I'm the owner. I'll give you the timber you need on condition that you give me twenty minutes of your time.' And he led both of them to faith in Jesus Christ, because he had earned the right to be heard. (Source unknown)

Watchman Nee, in his excellent book *Sit, Walk, Stand* shares an amazing story of forgiveness:

> I know of an old Japanese Christian woman who was disturbed by a thief who had broken into her house. In her simple but practical faith in the Lord, she cooked the man a meal – then offered him her keys. He was shamed by her action and God spoke to him. Through her testimony that man is a brother in Christ today.[1]

Of course, the results of obeying Christ by forgiving and going the extra mile don't always work out as well as the examples above. But it's very encouraging to know that the outcome of being forgiving can be so much more life-changing than when we refuse to forgive and try to take revenge. Not only are we transformed, but so is our witness to others.

Turn it around

In effect, Jesus says, 'Turn it around'. Ron tells the story of his father-in-law, Charles, who grew up in the Depression:

At eighteen years of age, he left home because his home situation with his relatives was so abusive. Sleeping under railway bridges in Australia, Charles got odd jobs and food where he could. When asked, 'Can you remember anything good about your father?' Charles replied, 'I cannot remember one positive thing about my dad.'

This boy's story had a happy ending though. He had found faith in Christ at around thirteen years of age. Later Charles made an important choice – which he shared with his children years afterwards: 'My family won't be like this!'

And he became an exceptional person, a brilliant dad, a man of love – his kids loved him, his grandchildren loved him and, before he died, he had the joy of being loved by his great-grandchildren also. Instead of perpetuating an abusive lifestyle and making his own children suffer in the way he had suffered, Charles chose to be different from his father. He lived in the opposite spirit.

The opposite spirit

Living in the opposite spirit means we face things differently; not in the way most people would. In practice, it means asking: 'Lord Jesus, what is on Your heart in this particular situation?' – then doing whatever He says.

We must remember that as Christians we have a spiritual enemy. The devil, the accuser Satan, wants to trap and damage us. He wants to cause us so much inner conflict that we get caught by an offence and then bound by *our reaction* to it. Part of Satan's strategy is to cause disunity: how he loves to alienate and isolate us as Christians! And how he loves us to dwell on the past, so that we never move on! Many Christians spend much of their lives thinking about an offence and wondering what they can do about it. They remember it very clearly. They nurture it; they rehearse it. Their whole life is one of being trapped by another situation, another person – and there is no freedom.

It's not easy to operate in the opposite spirit. We can't do it ourselves: we need God's help. As we have said before, it's very important in this process of forgiveness to recognise that forgiveness is '*a God thing*'. It is not natural to us. But it is natural to Him. Whoever we are and whatever stage of life we are in, God wants us to live a life of forgiveness. So we need to ask Him to provide His love and His Spirit for us to be able to truly forgive.

Remember: He wants to help and empower us to do just that.

Finally, let's take a moment to consider together:

What might my life look like in the future if I choose to live differently, asking God for His help to work through every issue of forgiveness as it arises, and trusting Him to turn these situations around for good?

Activity

Flick through the pages of a daily newspaper. You will probably find at least one story that could have had a very different ending if people had acted out of 'the opposite spirit'. How do you think the outcome might have changed if someone had chosen to forgive? Alternatively, as you watch familiar TV dramas or films (or read your favourite novel), review the action in the light of what you have learned. Can you see occasions where the plot might have drastically changed if someone had acted out of 'the opposite spirit'?

Reflection

- As you come to the end of this material, glance through the Reflections at the end of each chapter (and any notes you may have made), and remind yourself of points that have been especially important for you. How has this book helped you? How will you go forward now, as you apply these things to your life?
- In this chapter, we have seen how obedience to Christ in the area of forgiveness may have astonishing results. Think back to the timber yard story. What do you think the owner's attitude showed the robbers about God's love? Do you think

they would have spent time listening to the gospel if the owner had shouted, blamed and called the police? How does this challenge you, in regards to sharing the gospel with others?

- In Romans 12 we read that we must not be overcome by evil, but should 'overcome evil with good' (v21). The man in the timber yard effectively 'cut a deal' with the people who were robbing him. Has someone 'robbed' you in some way? Maybe financially, over an inheritance; or perhaps they have taken something else, such as your reputation, a relationship, or your choice in a matter. What might be some strategies for overcoming the evil that has been done to you?

If you are able to, why not close by praying this prayer:

Prayer

Lord, Your kingdom has been rightly called 'God's Upside-Down Kingdom'. I want to live an ongoing life of forgiveness. Help me to be open to Your conviction and leading when You want me to act in 'the opposite spirit' to that which we find in our world. Lord, I want to overcome evil with good, just as You did. I am trusting You to empower me to do this, by Your Spirit living in me. Thank You, Lord.
Amen.

You may find it helpful from time to time to review the principles of forgiveness which are summarised in Appendix 2.

Notes
1. Watchman Nee, *Sit, Walk, Stand* (Eastbourne: Kingsway, 1994) p33

Appendix 1

Reflections on Jesus' teaching on forgiveness

An eye for an eye

'He did this to me, so I'm going to do this to him. That's human nature, right? It's even in the Bible. Eye for eye, tooth for tooth...' True enough. But then Jesus came along and turned that 'natural justice' approach on its head.

Reading through the Scriptures, we can see that forgiveness is key in the ministry and life of Jesus. He *was* forgiveness personified. But we are not. And so we can find His teaching on the subject difficult to take, especially when we have been badly hurt ourselves. In Matthew 5:38–42, for instance, we read:

> You have heard that it was said, 'Eye for eye, and tooth for tooth.' But I tell you, Do not resist an evil person. If someone strikes you on the right cheek, turn to him the other also. And if someone wants to sue you and take your tunic, let him have your cloak as well. If someone forces you to go one mile, go with him two miles. Give to the one who asks you, and do not turn away from the one who wants to borrow from you.

Jesus is teaching something new and radical. We must, however, remember the actual context. He wasn't talking about major abuse – physical, sexual or emotional. Knocking someone's tooth out could be the result of a burst of anger; someone threw a punch and out came the tooth. He'd be hauled to the elders at the city gate and the victim would say 'He did this!' and the elders would reply, 'Well, you can take out his tooth, too.' This ancient law, the Law of Talion, common in a number of ancient Near East cultures, was designed to guide and limit revenge to the most appropriate penalty.

The Authorised Version translates it like this: 'whosoever shall smite thee on thy right cheek, turn to him the other also'. Think about that: if we are right-handed, we can't smite someone on the right cheek! (It is different if we are left-handed, of course.) The only way a right-handed person can do it is with a back-handed slap, so it was more like an insult, as in olden days when a man would take out his glove and smack someone across the face. So Jesus appears to be saying, 'If someone insults you by giving you a smack, or disrespecting you in some other way, don't respond.'

The second mile

Then Jesus continues, 'If someone forces you to go one mile, go with him two miles.' A soldier in those days could approach any civilian and say, 'Carry my pack for a mile' (literally *milion* – from the ancient Greek and Roman measurement of distance). And the civilian had to do it. So, what Jesus is actually saying is, 'Don't be the victim here. If you take control and say, "I'll do the second mile for you," you are back in control again. *He's* controlled the first mile and *you've* controlled the second mile.'

This illustrates the concept of regaining control when someone has offended us. In going the second mile, Jesus is teaching us that it's our decision to say, 'I'm not going to be controlled by that person any longer.' If we had to carry that pack, we could grumble that we've got to walk a mile back. Or we could go the second mile and say, 'I was in control of that. I gave it as a gift, a sacrifice.' To do that means we take back our power, rather than live in the bitterness of what was done to us. These examples are the 'easier end' of forgiveness.

A forgiving and forgiven heart

A forgiving heart is a requirement for a forgiven heart. In Matthew chapter 6, we read in the Lord's Prayer, 'Forgive us our debts, as we also have forgiven our debtors' (v12). It means, 'God, forgive me like I forgive others.' That's hard enough, but read on into verse 14: 'if you forgive men when they sin against you, your heavenly Father will also forgive you. *But if you don't forgive men their sins, your Father will not forgive your sins* [our italics].'

The truth is, when we move in the direction of forgiveness, we are put in a place where the fresh water of forgiveness will flow over *us*. Otherwise we will end up with a stagnant, poisonous pool of bitterness, hate, anger and revenge in our hearts.

In the Lord's Prayer, we can see that Jesus is really saying, 'If you really want to experience the freedom, then you have to come and say "God, this is too big for me but I do want to learn how to forgive. And I do want to come to the point where I can forgive the offence against me."'

Seventy times seven

There is spiritual power in both forgiving, and in not forgiving. This is illustrated well in Matthew 18:15–35, which we suggest you read.

In verses 15–20, we learn how to deal with a person who has sinned against us in the church. They might have gossiped, unfairly judged us, ignored us – or worse. We have to take the offender before the elders of our church. We might interpret this as an attitude of judgment, but it's reconciliation that Jesus is talking about here – sorting out the problem. And then, reading on into verse 21, we find Peter asking, 'Lord, how often should I forgive someone who sins against me? Seven times?' (NLT). Many of us would say, 'Being offended against seven times, and each time letting it go? No way!' But Jesus replies, 'Seventy-seven times.' Or, some translators think, 'Seventy times seven' (490) times! The parallel account in Luke 17:3–5 explains that the brother in the wrong has repented and asked for forgiveness seven times on the same day!

Jesus was not saying: 'OK, count up to seventy-seven (or 490) and when he does it one more time, kill the guy!' He intended us to have the attitude: 'There but for the grace of God go I. I need forgiveness; they need forgiveness.' Jesus wanted us *to realise how much we have been forgiven*. Amazingly, Jesus, the King of all kings, has forgiven us *everything*.

It is also worth noting that Peter wasn't talking about big issues such as physical or sexual abuse; he was talking about daily offences. Our own areas of struggle might be with these, but they may also be with much more damaging emotional hurts caused by desertion, abandonment, marital unfaithfulness, rejection and so on. Nevertheless, reaching a point where we are able to forgive can be very beneficial.

Appendix 2

Principles of forgiveness
Practical suggestions when forgiving an offender

1. Be convinced that God is a loving, forgiving God
- Are you confident that God loves you and has a forgiving attitude towards you?
  This is important because forgiveness, being difficult, will require His involvement and empowerment.

2. Clarify the particular offence(s) against you by this individual (or group)
- This is when you can 'own' in detail what actually occurred and how it affected you.
- Make a suitable time and place available in order to reflect on the offence(s), perhaps with a trusted confidant if the offence is a major influence in your life.
- This ownership may only be in your mind but you will find that it proves very powerful to speak it out also. To confess the offence(s) with words and to hear what you say brings clarity as well as a sense of ownership.
- Be very specific. What was/were the offence(s) and how has it/have they impacted your life?

3. Seek to understand the motive behind the offence(s)
- Was it accidental? Do you believe that the person did not really intend to hurt you?
- Was the offence malicious? Did the person set out to really damage you mentally, physically, spiritually or emotionally?

- Was the offence ongoing (occurring more than once and/or over a period of time)?
- Did you do something previously to cause this offence to take place?
- Is the offender aware that what he/she did was so hurtful to you?
- Do you know why the offence happened?
- Is this offence still occurring? (If so, and you sense being trapped by this, seek help from another trusted person.)

4. Understanding the impact of the offence
- In what ways have you changed as a result of what was done to you?
- How much of this change has been caused by the way you have dwelt on the hurtful events in your mind?
- What is your attitude to the offender now?
- Are you aware of anger, bitterness, thoughts of revenge, depression or other unhelpful thoughts or emotions?
- Why are you considering forgiveness now?
- Forgiveness involves facing the pain of the offence and moving past it. Are you prepared for this?

5. Seek a divine perspective
- After you have worked through the steps above, wait on God for His insight into the offence and its effects. Do not rush ahead. Seek His help and wisdom.
- Meditation on relevant scriptures may prove insightful.
- God's perspective may be different from your human point of view.
- The support and wisdom of a trusted friend may be helpful to you at this point. Often God uses others to speak to His children.

6. Releasing forgiveness
- Invite the Holy Spirit to give insight and empowerment as to how He wants you to proceed with forgiveness. Speaking it out will be part of it, but should you be alone for this? Do you need to be heard by someone you trust? Should the offender hear? Is a letter or email required? Should you buy a gift? And so on...
- As you sense that the timing for forgiving is right for you, you may begin to feel intense emotional pain. If so, you will need to choose not to allow this pain to prevent you from moving towards forgiving.
- The choice to forgive begins by naming the offences and the offender before God (preferably out loud).
- As a deliberate act of will, speak forgiveness towards the other person out loud. Remember, this is a *choice* not just a desire. Here is a suggestion:

Heavenly Father, I *choose* to forgive _____ [name] for _____ [the offence/s]. I ask you to release him/her from the guilt of what he/she did to me. Please heal me from the effects of that offence on my life. In Jesus' name. Amen.

(Guard against the temptation to water your prayer down so that it goes something like this: 'Lord Jesus *help me* to forgive _____ ' or, 'God, I *want* to forgive _____ '. This is a definite choice you are making, now.)

- Pray, offering forgiveness, seeking God's healing and asking for His blessing on the person who has been forgiven, if he/she is still living. Speaking out your forgiveness is important whether the offender is still living or not.

7. Reconciliation and rebuilding trust
*   Your act of forgiveness should only be discussed with the offender if he/she is aware of their offence and accepts their part in causing the problem. For this to be meaningful to the offender, it will be important for you to acknowledge any fault of your own if this is relevant.
*   If you confront the offender and he/she had no knowledge of the offence nor any intent to harm you, your forgiveness will be an unhelpful surprise. It may cause the offender unnecessary problems just as you are finding your own freedom. As a rule of thumb, if the offender is unaware of the offence and had no malice towards you in what he/she did, then simply share your forgiveness with a trusted independent party only. Deep forgiveness does not lose sight of the benefit it may bring to the offender.
*   When we have been offended and the other party owns his/her error, reconciliation is possible. Recognise that reconciliation is an offer that you may choose to pursue. Reconciliation may never be appropriate, for example, in cases of physical or sexual abuse.
*   Re-establishing trust is a deeper and much more difficult level of relational healing. It may never occur, but when it does, trust will be rebuilt slowly over a period of time.

Practical suggestions for finding forgiveness when I am the offender

1. Affirm the biblical truth that God is loving, understanding and forgiving

2. Acknowledge the offence to yourself – be specific

- Face up to exactly what you have done and own up to whom you have hurt in the process.

3. Confess to God and another trusted person – be specific and completely honest
- Guard against the tendency to excuse yourself by partly blaming others. Simply own *only* your contribution to the offence, even if you believe others were also at fault.
- This disclosure should also be made to the person offended if they are aware of the offence.
- Usually it is not appropriate to 'dump' new information on the person against whom one has offended, for example, 'I want you to know that I have hated you for the last ten years but God has convicted me of this and I have asked His forgiveness. I am sorry.'
- The situation where a spouse has been unfaithful and the other spouse does not appear to know is a different and more difficult circumstance altogether.

4. Pray for the mercy and grace of God to deal with your personal sin
- He has promised to respond to this prayer (Rom. 5:1–11).

5. Make restitution if this is relevant
- Pay back money and so on.

6. Be accountable and transparent with a trusted person of the same sex who is willing and able to see you through the process of starting again

7. Actively seek reconciliation if this is in the best interests of the offended party

- Where both appropriate and possible, restore relationships, firstly with God, then with others who have been offended by you.
- In cases of a serious offence, this is not appropriate and should not be considered.
- Reconciliation is never guaranteed – it is often an offer we make because, understandably, offended people do not always want to reconcile.
- Sometimes the other person has died or moved to an unknown location.
- Remember, however, that God is always seeking reconciliation with His children. His heart for us is reconciliation – with Himself and with others (see 2 Cor. 5:16–21).

8. Rebuild trust where appropriate
- The warnings given for reconciliation apply here also.
- Building trust is always a process and usually takes a long time.
- Following some offences, it is inappropriate to expect the level of trust to be restored to where it was before the offence, for example, child abuse, financial crimes, infidelity, untruthfulness.

9. Live as a forgiven person

Romans 8:1–17
Labelling yourself as a saved sinner is not helpful. The power to go forward is in the grace of God and the fact that you and I, despite our sins and failures, are His children by His choice.

Colossians 3:1–17

Put in place in your life new, biblical, helpful ways of thinking, behaving and choosing:

- concerning God
- concerning self
- concerning others

This requires a deliberate moving on; not remaining immobilised by the memories and experiences of sin(s) that have been forgiven. This may prove to be quite a struggle! Remember, this is not a minimisation of the wrongs committed. It is an embracing of the work of the cross of Christ and an application of the forgiveness of Jesus so that we may continue to be transformed into His likeness (2 Cor. 3:7–18).

Forgive! Life is too precious to be consumed by regrets, controlled by rage, or complicated by plans for revenge.

> To the Jews who had believed him, Jesus said, 'If you hold to my teaching, you are really my disciples. Then you will know the truth, and the truth will set you free.' (John 8:31–32)

> Jesus answered, 'I am the way and the truth and the life. No-one comes to the Father except through me.' (John 14:6)

This appendix is taken from the Life Issues series: *Forgiveness* by Ron Kallmier (Farnham: CWR, 2007). Used with permission.

Insight series

Handling issues that are often feared, ignored or misunderstood.

Courses

CWR's Insight courses draw on real-life case studies, biblical examples and counselling practices to offer insight on important topics, including depression, anxiety, stress, anger and self-acceptance. These courses have been developed by CWR's experienced tutors in response to the great need to help people understand and work through key issues.

These invaluable teaching days are designed both for those who would like to come for their own benefit and for those who seek to support or understand people facing particular issues.

To find out more and to book, visit **cwr.org.uk/courses** or call 01252 784719